T0320137

The Mechanics of Securitization

The Mechanics of Securitization

*A Practical Guide to Structuring
and Closing Asset-Backed
Security Transactions*

SULEMAN BAIG
MOORAD CHOUDHRY

WILEY

John Wiley & Sons, Inc.

Cover Design: John Wiley & Sons, Inc.

Cover Image: © Dynamic Graphics/Jupiter Images

For general information on our other products and services or for technical support, please contact our Customer Care Department within the United States at (800) 762-2974, outside the United States at (317) 572-3993 or fax (317) 572-4002.

Wiley publishes in a variety of print and electronic formats and by print-on-demand. Some material included with standard print versions of this book may not be included in e-books or in print-on-demand. If this book refers to media such as a CD or DVD that is not included in the version you purchased, you may download this material at http://booksupport.wiley.com. For more information about Wiley products, visit www.wiley.com.

Library of Congress Cataloging-in-Publication Data:

Baig, Suleman.

The mechanics of securitization: a practical guide to structuring and closing asset-backed security transactions/Suleman Baig, Moorad Choudhry.

  p. cm. — (Wiley finance series)

Includes bibliographical references and index.

ISBN 978-0-470-60972-9 (cloth); ISBN 978-1-118-22073-3 (ebk);

ISBN 978-1-118-25895-8 (ebk); ISBN 978-1-118-23454-9 (ebk)

1. Asset-backed financing. I. Baig, Suleman. II. Title.

HG4028.A84C46 2013

332.1'78—dc23   2012038292

Printed in the United States of America.

10 9 8 7 6 5 4 3 2 1

To my parents
— Suleman Baig

To a Solid Bond in Your Heart
— Moorad Choudhry

Contents

Foreword

It is regrettable that many of securitization's contributions to modern finance have been overshadowed by infamy since the financial crisis. While it has made for popular journalism to debate securitization in the abstract, there has been surprisingly little attempted commentary to actually explain what securitization is or does. Possibly, this is due to the fact that most pundits seem to underappreciate the regularity with which securitization techniques can be found in the financial system. The volume of securitized debt alone warrants more study and transparency in terms of the technology's inner workings. Thus, rather than discounting its utility, current thought leaders of finance (and certainly future students) would be best served by having better access to information around securitization's basic value proposition. Surely a more enlightened understanding would allow the debate to move beyond the rhetorical and reorient efforts toward identifying and deploying more practical uses of the technology. With that in mind, a book focused on explaining the basic mechanics of securitization is long overdue.

In its most basic form, a securitization vehicle acts as a small, single-purpose bank. As such, it plays the role of a financial intermediary between end borrowers and end investors. Where it does depart from a traditional bank, though, is in its balance sheet construct. Although it still finances itself by issuing debt and equity like a bank, its assets consist of a single, focused asset strategy. The single-purpose nature of its balance sheet is a distinct value creator for the financial system. It affords an investor the practical ability of taking exposure to a virtual bank that has a clearly defined risk mandate (financing only consumer loans, corporate loans, or real estate loans, for instance). In this regard, securitization is a uniquely powerful financial technology; it redefines the investible universe for investors and increases the options they have to diversify their portfolio risk. In the context of an overall portfolio investment strategy, the ability to take "pure" asset class exposure provides for better risk calibration and more flexibility for investors to shape their targeted risk-return profiles.

The aforementioned diversification benefit made available to an individual investor can be expanded into a global context. Prior to the availability of securitization, the realistic ability of a lender to diversify globally was limited by practical access to foreign markets. Though a regionally concentrated lender may want to diversify its loan book, a lack of origination infrastructure in the new market would deem it prohibitive. Given such practical constraints, the lender would be limited to only indirect methods, which would mean either purchasing a stake in a foreign lender or sourcing a loan participation. The former approach lacks asset-class risk clarity and brings risks perhaps far beyond what the lender had initially desired (as it captures the foreign banks' entire business). The latter is restrictive in that it typically only works for exposures to large corporate loans (i.e., ones that can be parsed and syndicated). The fact that it "practically" allows for regionally sourced risk to be diversified with clearly defined alternative asset exposure makes securitization a key lever in reducing overall global systemic risk.

For both the individual and global examples, however, one needs to be careful not to confuse risk dispersion with risk transformation: Securitization in itself does not change the risk of an underlying asset class. This has been the biggest challenge with how securitization has been falsely characterized and hence tainted in the context of the U.S. subprime mortgage market. It is incorrect to suggest, as some have, that it was the securitization technology in itself that caused the losses experienced by global investors. In the end, securitization was only the vehicle by which investors chose to take exposure to the U.S. subprime mortgage asset class. It was the flawed understanding and choice of asset class that caught out the affected participants (originators, investors, rating agencies, and regulators).

The lesson is very clear from this experience: One should not forget that securitization is only a tool. And as with all tools, users need to understand its purpose so it can be used effectively, and most importantly, appropriately.

For the skeptic, it is also important to recognize how mainstream securitization technology has become. As a start, one only needs to look at the magnitude with which central banks have utilized the technology. For instance, securitized debt (asset-backed securities, covered bonds, and so on) has been the primary source of collateral used to back the liquidity provision made to the monetary system. For that matter, the European Financial Stability Facility, established to provide financial assistance to euro area member states, is built on the back of securitization technology. Specifically, the EFSF borrows from the capital markets on the back of collateral (i.e., security) provided by a portfolio of guarantee commitments from euro area members. Interestingly, the most notable example is the German Pfandbrief market; it is believed to be the oldest securitized market and has been in operation for approximately 200 years. Perhaps ironically, the principal underlying collateral in this market is personal home mortgages, and it is still the largest source of funding for German banks to this day.

More generally though, securitization principles can be found in any circumstance where there exists a financial obligation and such obligation's creditworthiness is enhanced by the contribution of collateral. The collateral afforded can take many forms, of course (financial assets, property rights, future revenue streams). All these forms can serve as further consideration to help strengthen an outstanding general promise to repay debt. The pledging of collateral to reshape the credit risk profile for a lender is a basic fundamental principle of securitization, and examples of its use are evident throughout the fixed income landscape (municipal revenue bonds, high-yield bonds, bank loans, repurchase obligations).

One might ask, "Why are the borrowers in these markets willing to pledge security against their debt?" In simple terms, it is all about optimizing risk and return between different borrowers and lenders. By offering collateral, the borrower will generally benefit by getting better loan terms. Equally, the borrower will often be able to attract more willing lenders to offer the same loan (i.e., better pricing and capacity). This example should be familiar to anyone who has purchased a home with a mortgage; the smaller the size of the mortgage relative to the value of the home (the collateral in this instance), the better the mortgage terms and overall availability. I have used this simple example purposefully; it highlights how germane securitization concepts are, even in our personal lives.

I suspect practitioners of securitization would question my use of a single loan, or single secured borrowing, as the basis for framing securitization mechanics. This is not surprising, given that most industry participants assimilate securitization with the packaging of large numbers of small individual loans. If one steps back, however, and truly looks at the basics of what securitization does, it's simply a scalable version of the secured lending business. Secured borrowing is an old technology that predates the term "securitization" and is in itself a simple technology. In fact, it is not surprising that it is in use today, given that the concept has been used throughout history by individuals, corporations, and government borrowers alike. I suppose what is new is the fact that in today's high-tech world it can be scaled. The advent of computer technology during the tail end of the last century is what has enabled secured borrowing to be industrialized, hence warranting its own nomenclature. Without computers, it would not be easy for loan originators to efficiently aggregate and track large numbers of loans such that they could be financed or sold in bulk.

In the end, words at times attract a connotation that drifts away from their intended meaning. I would suggest the inappropriate negative connotation ascribed to securitization is misplaced in this way. Like many new technologies introduced during the industrial revolution, securitization is simply a more efficient version of an old technology. In a world where loans are generally no longer recorded in paper format nor are they decisioned in a bank branch, it is not surprising that the way they are financed should evolve as well. So, as one proceeds through the text of this worthwhile book, one should take due care to truly understand the specific workings of securitization-based financing. As mentioned previously, many of securitization's basic features are quite mainstream and are not as obscure as its name suggests.

Securitization has a genuine role to play in the global financial system and will not disappear. One needs only to reflect on experiences of other markets for context (e.g., the junk bond market of 1980s, the high-tech bubble of 1990s): These markets didn't disappear, either. And like securitization of the 2000s, each of these episodes can make the financial markets stronger, provided we take a lesson from them and act on the message.

Oldrich Masek
Managing Director
JPMorgan Chase
October 23, 2012

Preface

In 2009 *The Times* newspaper of London carried an interview with Paul Volcker. The former chairman of the Federal Reserve "berated bankers for their failure to acknowledge a problem with personal rewards and questioned their claims for financial innovation." According to *The Times*, Mr. Volcker rebuked "senior figures in the financial world for failing to grasp the magnitude of the financial crisis and belittled their suggested reforms." As bankers demanded that new regulation should not stifle innovation, Mr. Volcker was quoted as saying, "The biggest innovation in the industry over the past 20 years has been the cash machine."

It's a pity that this impression is now fairly commonplace in business, media, and political circles. One only has to look at the mobile telephone industry, and to be aware that it was financed mainly by recourse to financial engineering techniques that included securitization, to understand that innovation in finance has often been a force for much good in the world. It is worthy of preservation, and if one was to observe a rickshaw puller on the streets of Dhaka, Bangladesh (average salary $1 per day) using a cell phone, one would indeed be convinced of this. The technology needed to make the cell phone available to a mass population worldwide required hundreds of billions of dollars in investment, and a fair proportion of these funds were raised via the securitization markets.

This book is not a general textbook on banking or finance, much less a polemic on the virtues of free markets and capitalism. It is a very focused guide aimed at practitioners in structured finance who are involved with originating, structuring, or arranging securitization transactions. Essentially it has been written to act as a checklist of necessary tasks for commercial banks that are interested in closing a securitization of assets either off their own balance sheet or on behalf of a third-party bank. These assets might be corporate loans, mortgages, credit card loans, or other more esoteric "future flow" cash receivables, but the essential principles that must be followed when securitizing any asset class are virtually identical, and differ only in detail. These essential principles are covered here. Much securitization activity in the immediate post-2008 era was of the "in-house" variety, with an objective of creating tradeable securities that could then be used as collateral when obtaining funding from their central bank. The templates in this book are of equal application to someone planning such a transaction.

Ultimately we hope this book is of most value to practitioners looking to close a securitization deal for the first time, and for whom the checklist format of this book is intended to act as a project management guide.

ORGANIZATION OF THE BOOK

This book is organized into three parts. Part One is a primer for those wishing an introduction to securitization and asset-backed securities (ABS), and contains two chapters. Chapter 1 is the primer and Chapter 2 is an assessment of the impact of the 2008 bank crash. In Part Two we discuss the structuring and execution of an ABS transaction, and the rating agency and legal review requirements. The contents of Part Two are designed to act as a checklist and template, and can be readily applied by commercial banks looking to undertake their own securitization transactions.

Part Three uses templates, checklists, and pro forma documents from an actual corporate loans ABS deal to provide color to the text in Part Two.

The authors welcome comments or review critique, which should be sent to them via John Wiley & Sons Limited.

Suleman Baig
Moorad Choudhry
London
June 2012

Acknowledgments

We would like to thank Laurence Rickard and Eric Eastlund for their input and assistance. Both, along with Nicholas Dibley, are confirmed Jedis of securitization.

Thanks also to Stuart Turner, Mark Burgess, Maira Chatziperou, Dan Cunningham, Gino Landuyt, Paul Kerlogue, Anne Azencot, Sharad Samy, the legendary Jim Croke, and Khurram Butt for their invaluable help and input during the work that went into the series of structured finance transactions that were Picaros Funding PLC (*Euromoney* Structured Finance Deal of the Year for 2005), Calculus Master Series Limited, Castafiore Fund Limited, and Red Sea Master Series Limited.

Fans of George Remi will detect a pattern here . . .

The Mechanics of Securitization

One

Introduction to Securitization

The purpose of this book is essentially to act as a guide, and checklist, for bankers wishing to originate and close a securitization transaction, either in-house or on behalf of a third-party client bank. Before that, however, we wish to place this template in context by beginning with some descriptive background on the market and its products.

To that end, Part One is an introduction to the concept of securitization, and would be of value to newcomers to the market and graduate students in finance. It defines the key elements behind the technique, and also illustrates the principles of securitization as a generic concept. Chapter 2 looks at some examples of the impact of the 2008 financial crash on the market.

CHAPTER 1

Introduction to Securitization and Asset-Backed Securities

Perhaps the best illustration of the flexibility, innovation, and user-friendliness of the debt capital markets is the rise in the use and importance of securitization. As defined in Sundaresan (1997, page 359), securitization is "a framework in which some illiquid assets of a corporation or a financial institution are transformed into a package of securities backed by these assets, through careful packaging, credit enhancements, liquidity enhancements, and structuring."

The flexibility of securitization is a key advantage for both issuers and investors. Financial engineering techniques employed by investment banks today enable bonds to be created from any type of cash flow. The most typical such flows are those generated by high-volume loans such as residential mortgages and car and credit card loans, which are recorded as assets on bank or financial house balance sheets. In a securitization, the loan assets are packaged together, and their interest payments are used to service the new bond issue.

In addition to the more traditional cash flows from mortgages and loan assets, investment banks underwrite bonds secured with flows received by leisure and recreational facilities, such as health clubs, and other entities, such as nursing homes. Bonds securitizing mortgages are usually treated as a separate class, termed *mortgage-backed securities,* or MBSs. Those with other underlying assets are known as *asset-backed securities,* or ABSs. The type of asset class backing a securitized bond issue determines the method used to analyze and value it.

The asset-backed market represents a large and diverse group of securities suited to a varied group of investors. Often these instruments are the only way for institutional investors to pick up yield while retaining assets with high credit ratings. They are considered by issuers because they represent a cost-effective means of removing assets from their balance sheets, thus freeing up lines of credit and enabling them to access lower-cost funding.

Instruments are available backed by a variety of assets covering the entire yield curve, with either fixed or floating coupons. In the United Kingdom, for example, it is common for mortgage-backed bonds to have floating coupons, mirroring the interest basis of the country's mortgages. To suit investor requirements, however, some of these structures have been modified, through swap arrangements, to pay fixed coupons.

The market in structured finance securities was hit hard in the wake of the 2007–2008 financial crisis. Investors shunned asset-backed securities in a mass flight to quality. As the global economy recovered from recession, interest in securitization resumed. We examine the fallout in the market later in this chapter. First we discuss the principal concepts that drive the desire to undertake securitization.

THE CONCEPT OF SECURITIZATION

Securitization is a well-established practice in the global debt capital markets. It refers to the sale of assets, which generate cash flows, from the institution that owns them, to another company that has been specifically set up for the purpose, and the issuing of notes by this second company. These notes are backed by the cash flows from the original assets. The technique was introduced first as a means of funding for mortgage banks in the United States, with the first such transaction generally recognized as having been undertaken by Salomon Brothers in 1979. Subsequently, the technique was applied to other assets such as credit card payments and leasing receivables, and has been employed worldwide. It has also been employed as part of asset-liability management, as a means of managing balance sheet risk.

Reasons for Undertaking Securitization

The driving force behind securitization has been the need for banks to realize value from the assets on their balance sheet. Typically these assets are residential mortgages, corporate loans, and retail loans such as credit card debt. The following are factors that might lead a financial institution to securitize a part of its balance sheet:

- If revenues received from assets remain roughly unchanged but the size of assets has decreased, this will lead to an increase in the return on equity ratio.
- The level of capital required to support the balance sheet will be reduced, which again can lead to cost savings or allow the institution to allocate the capital to other, perhaps more profitable, business.

■ The financial institution can obtain cheaper funding: Frequently the interest payable on ABS securities is considerably below the level payable on the underlying loans. This creates a cash surplus for the originating entity.

In other words, a bank will securitize part of its balance sheet for one or all of the following reasons:

■ Funding the assets it owns
■ Balance sheet capital management
■ Risk management and credit risk transfer.

We consider each of these in turn.

Funding Banks can use securitization to (1) support rapid asset growth, (2) diversify their funding mix and reduce cost of funding, and (3) reduce maturity mismatches. All banks will not wish to be reliant on only a single or a few sources of funding, as this can be risky in times of market liquidity difficulty. Banks aim to optimize their funding between a mix of retail, interbank, and wholesale sources. Securitization has a key role to play in this mix. It also enables a bank to reduce its funding costs. This is because the securitization process separates the credit rating of the originating institution from the credit rating of the issued notes. Typically most of the notes issued by special purpose vehicles (SPVs) will be more highly rated than the bonds issued directly by the originating bank itself. Although the liquidity of the secondary market in ABSs is frequently lower than that of the corporate bond market, and this adds to the yield payable by an ABS, it is frequently the case that the cost to the originating institution of issuing debt is still lower in the ABS market because of the latter's higher rating. Finally, there is the issue of maturity mismatches. The business of bank asset-liability management (ALM) is inherently one of maturity mismatch, because a bank often funds long-term assets, such as residential mortgages, with short-asset liabilities, such as bank account deposits or interbank funding. This funding "gap" can be mitigated via securitization, as the originating bank receives funding from the sale of the assets, and the economic maturity of the issued notes frequently matches that of the assets.

Balance Sheet Capital Management Banks use securitization to improve balance sheet capital management. This provides (1) regulatory capital relief, in some cases (depending on the form of the transaction), (2) "economic" capital relief, and (3) diversified sources of funding. As stipulated in the Bank for International Settlements (BIS) capital rules,[1] also known as the Basel rules, banks must maintain a minimum capital level for their assets, in relation to the risk of these assets. Under Basel I, for every $100 of risk-weighted assets a bank must hold at least $8 of capital; however, the designation of each asset's risk-weighting is restrictive. For example, with the exception of mortgages, customer loans are 100 percent risk weighted regardless of the underlying rating of the borrower or the quality of the security held. The anomalies that this raises, which need not concern us here, were partly addressed by the Basel II rules, which became effective from 2007. However, the Basel rules that have been in place since 1988 (and effective from 1992) were a key driver of securitization. Because an SPV is not a bank, it is not subject to Basel rules, and needs only such capital as is economically required by the nature of the assets it contains. This is not a set amount, but is significantly below the 8 percent level required by banks in all cases. Although an originating bank does not obtain 100 percent regulatory capital relief when it sells assets off its balance sheet to an SPV where it will have retained a first-loss piece out of the issued notes, its regulatory capital charge may be significantly reduced after the securitization.[2]

To the extent that securitization provides regulatory capital relief, it can be thought of as an alternative to capital raising, compared with the traditional sources of Tier 1 (equity), preferred shares, and perpetual loan notes with step-up coupon features. By reducing the amount of capital that has to be used to support the asset pool, a bank can also improve its return-on-equity (ROE) value. This will be received favorably by shareholders.

Risk Management   Once assets have been securitized, the credit risk exposure on these assets for the originating bank is reduced considerably and, if the bank does not retain a first-loss capital piece (the most junior of the issued notes), it is removed entirely. This is because assets have been sold to the SPV. Securitization can also be used to remove nonperforming assets from banks' balance sheets. This has the dual advantage of removing credit risk and removing a potentially negative sentiment from the balance sheet, as well as freeing up regulatory capital as before. Further, there is a potential upside from securitizing such assets: If any of them start performing again, or there is a recovery value obtained from defaulted assets, the originator will receive any surplus profit made by the SPV.

---

[1]For further information on this, see Choudhry (2007).

[2]The "first loss" piece refers to the most junior tranche on the liabilities sides of the securitization (the issued notes), and is the tranche that is exposed to the first of any default losses suffered by the underlying asset pool. In other words, it carries the most performance risk for the investor.

Potential Benefits of Securitization to Investors

In theory there are a number of benefits available to investors from investing in ABS notes, centered mainly on the alternative sectors that they allow investors to diversify into. The potential attractions include:

- Ability to diversify into sectors of exposure that might not be available in the regular bond markets (for example, residential mortgages or project finance loans).
- Access to different (and sometimes superior) risk-reward profiles.
- Access to sectors that are otherwise not open to them.

A key benefit of ABS notes is the ability to tailor risk-return profiles. For example, if there is a lack of assets of any specific credit rating, these can be created via securitization. Securitized notes sometimes produce a better risk-reward performance than corporate bonds of the same rating and maturity. Although this might seem peculiar (why should one AA-rated bond perform better in terms of credit performance than another just because it is asset backed?), this occurs because the originator holds the first-loss piece in the structure.

A holding in an ABS also diversifies investor risk exposure. For example, rather than invest $100 million in an AA-rated corporate bond and be exposed to event risk associated with the issuer, investors can gain exposure to, for instance, 100 pooled assets. These pooled assets will, in theory, have lower concentration risk, although the experience of 2007–2008 showed that this theoretical diversification of concentration did not always occur in practice.

THE PROCESS OF SECURITIZATION

We look now at the process of securitization, the nature of the SPV structure, and issues such as credit enhancements and the cash flow waterfall.

Securitization Process

The securitization process involves a number of participants. First there is the *originator*, the firm whose assets are being securitized. The most common process involves an *issuer* acquiring the assets from the originator. The issuer is usually a company that has been specially set up for the purpose of the securitization, which is the SPV and is usually domiciled offshore. The creation of an SPV ensures that the underlying asset pool is held separate from the other assets of the originator. This is done so that in the event that the originator is declared bankrupt or insolvent, the assets that have been transferred to the SPV will not be affected. This is known as being "bankruptcy remote." Conversely, if the underlying assets begin to deteriorate in quality and are subject to a ratings downgrade, investors have no recourse to the originator.

By holding the assets within an SPV framework, defined in formal legal terms, the financial status and credit rating of the originator becomes almost irrelevant to the bondholders. The process of securitization often involves *credit enhancements*, in which a third-party guarantee of credit quality is obtained, so that notes issued under the securitization are often rated at investment grade and up to AAA-grade.

The process of structuring a securitization deal ensures that the liability side of the SPV—the issued notes—carries lower cost than the asset side of the SPV. This enables the originator to secure lower-cost funding that it would not otherwise be able to obtain in the unsecured market. This is a tremendous benefit for institutions with lower credit ratings

Exhibit 1.1 illustrates the process of securitization in simple fashion.

Mechanics of Securitization   Securitization involves a true sale of the underlying assets from the balance sheet of the originator. This is why a separate legal entity, the SPV, is created to act as the issuer of the notes. The assets being securitized are sold onto the balance sheet of the SPV. The process involves:

- Undertaking due diligence on the quality and future prospects of the assets.
- Setting up the SPV and then effecting the transfer of assets to it.
- Underwriting of loans for credit quality and servicing.
- Determining the structure of the notes, including how many tranches are to be issued, in accordance to originator and investor requirements.
- The notes being rated by one or more credit rating agencies.
- The placing of notes in the capital markets.

The sale of assets to the SPV needs to be undertaken so that it is recognized as a true legal transfer. The originator will usually hire external legal counsel to advise it in such matters. The credit rating process will consider the character and quality of the assets, and also whether any enhancements have been made to the assets that will raise their credit quality. This can include *overcollateralization,* which is when the principal value of notes issued is lower than the principal value of assets, and a liquidity facility is provided by a bank.

EXHIBIT 1.1   The securitization process

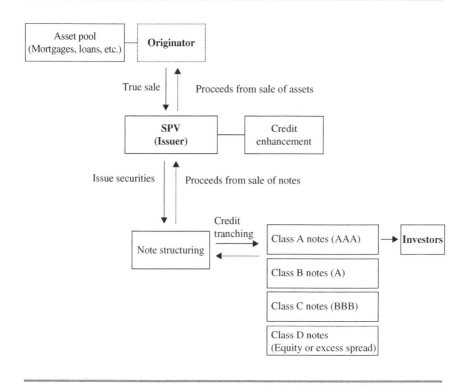

A key consideration for the originator is the choice of the underwriting bank that structures the deal and places the notes. The originator will award the mandate for its deal to an investment bank on the basis of fee levels, marketing ability, and track record with assets being securitized.

Securitization Note Tranching   As illustrated in Exhibit 1.1, in a securitization the issued notes are structured to reflect specified risk areas of the asset pool, and thus are rated differently. The senior tranche is usually rated AAA. The lower-rated notes usually have an element of *overcollateralization* and are thus capable of absorbing losses. The most junior note is the lowest rated or nonrated. It is often referred to as the *first-loss piece*, because it is impacted by losses in the underlying asset pool first. The first-loss piece is sometimes called the *equity piece* or equity note (even though it is a bond) and is usually held by the originator.

Financial Modeling   The originator will construct a cash flow model to estimate the size of the issued notes. The model will consider historical sales values, any seasonal factors in sales, credit card cash flows, and so on. Certain assumptions will be made when constructing the model, for example growth projections, inflation levels, tax levels, and so on. The model will consider a number of different scenarios, and also calculate the minimum asset coverage levels required to service the issued debt. A key indicator in the model will be the debt service coverage ratio (DSCR). The more conservative the DSCR, the more comfort there will be for investors in the notes. For a residential mortgage deal, this ratio might be approximately 2.5 to 3.0; however, for an exotic asset class like an airline ticket receivables deal, the DSCR would be unlikely to be lower than 4.0. The model will therefore calculate the amount of notes that can be issued against the assets while maintaining the minimum DSCR.

Credit Rating   It is common for securitization deals to be rated by one or more of the formal credit ratings agencies such as Moody's, Fitch, or Standard & Poor's. A formal credit rating will make it easier for the originator to place the notes with investors. The methodology employed by the ratings agencies takes into account both qualitative and quantitative factors, and will differ according to the asset class being securitized. The main issues in a typical ABS deal include:

- Corporate credit quality: These are risks associated with the originator, and are factors that affect its ability to continue operations, meet its financial obligations, and provide a stable foundation for generating future receivables. This might be analyzed according to (1) the issuer's historical financial performance, including its liquidity and debt structure; (2) its status within its domicile country, for example whether it is state-owned; (3) the general economic conditions for industry and for airlines; and (4) the historical record and current state of the airline—for instance its safety record and age of its airplanes.
- The competition and industry trends: the issuer's market share, the competition on its network.
- Regulatory issues, such as need for the issuer to comply with forthcoming legislation that would impact its cash flows.
- Legal structure of the SPV and transfer of assets.
- Cash flow analysis.

Based on the findings of the ratings agency, the arranger may redesign some aspect of the deal structure so that the issued notes are rated at the required level.

Above is a summary of the key issues involved in the process of securitization. Depending on investor sentiment, market conditions, and legal issues, the process from inception to closure of the deal may take anything from three to 12 months or more. After the notes have been issued, the arranging bank will no longer have anything to do with the issue; however, the bonds themselves require a number of agency services for their remaining life until they mature or are paid off. These agency services include paying agent, cash manager, and custodian.

SPV Structures

There are essentially two main securitization structures: amortizing (pass-through) and revolving. A third type, the master trust, is used by frequent issuers.

Amortizing Structures Amortizing structures pay principal and interest to investors on a coupon-by-coupon basis throughout the life of the security, as illustrated in Exhibit 1.1. They are priced and traded based on expected maturity and weighted-average life (WAL), which is the time-weighted period during which principal is outstanding. A WAL approach incorporates various prepayment assumptions, and any change in this prepayment speed will increase or decrease the rate at which principal is repaid to investors. Pass-through structures are commonly used in residential and commercial mortgage-backed deals (RMBS and CMBS) and consumer loan ABS.

Revolving Structures Revolving structures revolve the principal of the assets; that is, during the revolving period, principal collections are used to purchase new receivables that fulfill the necessary criteria. The structure is used for short-dated assets with a relatively high prepayment speed, such as credit card debt and auto loans. During the amortization period, principal payments are paid to investors in a series of equal installments (*controlled amortization*) or principal is "trapped" in a separate account until the expected maturity date and then paid in a single lump sum to investors (*soft bullet*).

Master Trust Frequent issuers under U.S. and UK law use *master trust* structures, which allow multiple securitizations to be issued from the same SPV. Under such schemes, the originator transfers assets to the master trust SPV. Notes are then issued out of the asset pool based on investor demand. Master trusts have been used by MBS and credit card ABS originators.

Credit Enhancement

Credit enhancement refers to the group of measures that can be instituted as part of the securitization process for ABS and MBS issues so that the credit rating of the issued notes meets investor requirements. The lower the quality of the assets being securitized, the greater the need for credit enhancement. This is often by one of the following methods:

Overcollateralization: Where the nominal value of the assets in the pool is in excess of the nominal value of issued securities.

Pool insurance: An insurance policy provided by an insurance company to cover the risk of principal loss in the collateral pool. The claims-paying rating of the insurance company is important in determining the overall rating of the issue.

Senior/junior note classes: Credit enhancement is provided by subordinating a class of notes (class B notes) to the senior class notes (class A notes). The class B notes' right to their proportional share of cash flows is subordinated to the rights of the senior noteholders. Class B notes do not receive payments of principal until certain rating agency requirements have been met; specifically, satisfactory performance of the collateral pool over a predetermined period, or in many cases until all of the senior note classes have been redeemed in full.

Margin step-up: A number of ABS issues incorporate a step-up feature in the coupon structure, which typically coincides with a call date. Although the issuer is usually under no obligation to redeem the notes at this point, the step-up feature was introduced as an added incentive for investors and serves to imply from the outset that the economic cost of paying a higher coupon is unacceptable, and so the issuer will seek to refinance by exercising its call option.

Excess spread: This is the difference between the return on the underlying assets and the interest rate payable on the issued notes (liabilities). The monthly excess spread is used to cover expenses and any losses. If any surplus is left over, it is held in a reserve account to cover against future losses or (if not required for that) as a benefit to the originator. In the meantime, the reserve account is a credit enhancement for investors.

All securitization structures incorporate a *cash waterfall* process, whereby the cash that is generated by the asset pool is paid in order of payment priority. Only when senior obligations have been met can more junior obligations be paid. An independent third-party agent is usually employed to run tests on the vehicle to confirm that there is sufficient cash available to pay all obligations. If a test is failed, then the vehicle will start to pay off the notes, starting from the senior notes. The waterfall process is illustrated in Exhibit 1.2.

EXHIBIT 1.2   Cash flow waterfall (priority of payments)

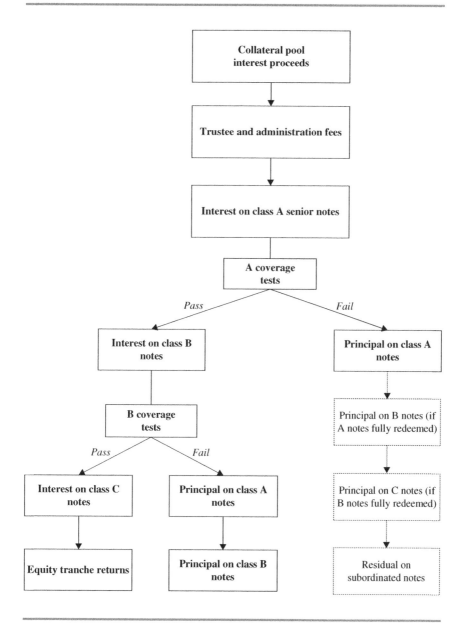

EXAMPLE 1.1: IMPACT ON BALANCE SHEET

The exhibit in this example illustrates by a hypothetical example the effect on the liability side of an originating bank's balance sheet from a securitization transaction. Following the process, selected assets have been removed from the balance sheet, although the originating bank may have retained the first-loss piece. With regard to the regulatory capital impact, this first-loss amount is deducted from the bank's total capital position. For example, assume a bank has $100 million of risk-weighted assets and a target Basel ratio of 12 percent,[3] and securitizes all $100 million of these assets. It retains the first-loss tranche, which forms 1.5 percent of the total issue. The remaining 98.5 percent will be sold on to the market. The bank will still have to set aside 1.5 percent of capital as a buffer against future losses, but it has been able to free itself of the remaining 10.5 percent of capital.

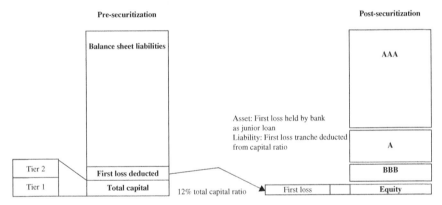

Regulatory capital impact of securitization

SECURITIZING MORTGAGES

A mortgage is a long-term loan taken out to purchase residential or commercial property, which itself serves as security for the loan. The term of the loan is usually 20 to 25 years, but a shorter period is possible if the borrower, or *mortgagor,* wishes one. In exchange for the right to use the property during the term of the mortgage, the borrower provides the lender, or *mortgagee,* with a *lien,* or claim, against the property and agrees to make regular

---

[3]The minimum is 8 percent, but many banks set aside an amount well in excess of this minimum required level.

payments of both principal and interest. If the borrower defaults on the interest payments, the lender has the right to take over and sell the property, recovering the loan from the proceeds of the sale. The lien is removed when the debt is paid off.

A lending institution may have many hundreds of thousands of individual residential and commercial mortgages on its books. When these are pooled together and used as collateral for a bond issue, the result is an MBS. In the U.S. market, certain mortgage-backed securities were backed, either implicitly or explicitly, by the government. A government agency, the Government National Mortgage Association (GNMA, known as Ginnie Mae), and two government-sponsored agencies, the Federal Home Loan Mortgage Corporation and the Federal National Mortgage Association (Freddie Mac and Fannie Mae, respectively), purchased mortgages to pool and hold in their portfolios and, possibly, securitize. The MBSs created by these agencies traded essentially as risk-free instruments and were not rated by the credit agencies. Following the 2007–2008 financial crash, Fannie Mae and Freddie Mac were taken under explicit government control.

Mortgage-backed bonds not issued by government agencies are rated in the same way as other corporates. Some nongovernment agencies obtain mortgage insurance for their issues to boost their credit quality. The credit rating of the insurer then becomes an important factor in the bond's credit rating.

Growth of the Market

We list the following features of mortgage-backed bonds:

- Their yields were traditionally higher than those of corporate bonds with the same credit rating. In the mid-1990s, mortgage-backed bonds traded around 100 to 200 basis points above Treasury bonds; by comparison, corporates traded at a spread of around 80 to 150 for bonds of similar credit quality. This yield gap stems from the mortgage bonds' complexity and the uncertainty of mortgage cash flows. At the height of the structured finance market in 2007, MBS securities rated AAA paid a comfortable 20 to 30 bps over government security. That this was underpriced is reflected in spreads post-2008, which remain higher by some margin over equivalent rated conventional securities.
- They offer investors a wider range of maturities, cash flows, and security collateral to choose from.
- The market is large and until the 2007 crash was very liquid; agency mortgage-backed bonds had the same liquidity as Treasury bonds. Post-2008 the liquidity reduced considerably.

▓ Unlike most other bonds, mortgage-backed securities pay monthly coupons, an advantage for investors who require frequent income payments.

EXAMPLE 1.2: SECURITIZATION TRANSACTION

We illustrate the impact of securitizing the balance sheet under original Basel I regulatory rules using a hypothetical example from ABC Bank PLC.

The bank has a mortgage book of £100 million, and the regulatory weight for this asset is 50 percent. The capital requirement is therefore £4 million (that is, 8 percent × 0.5 percent × £100 million). The capital is composed of equity, estimated to cost 25 percent, and subordinated debt, which has a cost of 10.2 percent. The cost of straight debt is 10 percent. The ALM desk reviews a securitization of 10 percent of the asset book, or £10 million. The loan book has a fixed duration of 20 years, but its effective duration is estimated at seven years, due to refinancings and early repayment. The net return from the loan book is 10.2 percent.

The ALM desk decides on a securitized structure that is made up of two classes of security, subordinated notes and senior notes. The subordinated notes will be granted a single-A rating due to their higher risk, whereas the senior notes are rated triple-A. Given such ratings the required rate of return for the subordinated notes is 10.61 percent, and that of the senior notes is 9.80 percent. The senior notes have a lower cost than the current balance sheet debt, which has a cost of 10 percent. To obtain a single-A rating, the subordinated notes need to represent at least 10 percent of the securitized amount. The costs associated with the transaction are the initial cost of issue and the yearly servicing cost, estimated at 0.20 percent of the securitized amount (see the accompanying summary information).

ABC Bank PLC mortgage loan book
and securitization proposal

Current funding	
Cost of equity	25%
Cost of subordinated debt	10.20%
Cost of debt	10%
Mortgage book	
Net yield	10.20%
Duration	7 years
Balance outstanding	£100 million
Proposed structure	
Securitized amount	£10 million

Senior securities:	
Cost	9.80%
Weighting	90%
Maturity	10 years
Subordinated notes:	
Cost	10.61%
Weighting	10%
Maturity	10 years
Servicing costs	0.20%

A bank's cost of funding is the average cost of all the funds it employed. The funding structure in our example is capital 4 percent, divided into 2 percent equity at 25 percent, 2 percent subordinated debt at 10.20 percent, and 96 percent debt at 10 percent. The weighted funding cost F therefore is:

$$F_{\text{balance sheet}} = (96\% \times 10\%) + [(8\% \times 50\%) \times (25\% \times 50\%) + (10.20\% \times 50\%)]$$
$$= 10.30\%$$

This average rate is consistent with the 25 percent before-tax return on equity given at the start. If the assets do not generate this return, the received return will change accordingly, because it is the end result of the bank's profitability. As currently the assets generate only 10.20 percent, they are performing below shareholder expectations. The return actually obtained by shareholders is such that the average cost of funds is identical to the 10.20 percent return on assets. We may calculate this return to be:

$$\text{Asset return} = 10.20\% = (96\% \times 10\%) + (8\% \times 50\%)$$
$$\times (\text{ROE} \times 50\% + 10.20\% \times 50\%)$$

Solving this relationship we obtain a return on equity of 19.80 percent, which is lower than shareholder expectations. In theory, the bank would find it impossible to raise new equity in the market because its performance would not compensate shareholders for the risk they are incurring by holding the bank's paper. Therefore, any asset that is originated by the bank would have to be securitized, which would also be expected to raise the shareholder return.

The ALM desk proceeds with the securitization, issuing £9 million of the senior securities and £1 million of the subordinated notes. The bonds are placed by an investment bank with institutional investors. The outstanding balance of the loan book decreases from £100 million to £90 million. The weighted assets are therefore £45 million. Therefore, the capital requirement for the loan book is now £3.6 million, a reduction from the original capital requirement by £400,000, which can be used for expansion in another area, a possible route for which is given here.

Impact of securitization on balance sheet

Outstanding balances	Value (£m)	Capital required (£m)
Initial loan book	100	4
Securitized amount	10	0.4
Senior securities	9	Sold
Subordinated notes	1	Sold
New loan book	90	3.6
Total assets	90	
Total weighted assets	45	3.6

The benefit of the securitization is the reduction in the cost of funding. The funding cost as a result of securitization is the weighted cost of the senior notes and the subordinated notes, together with the annual servicing cost. The cost of the senior securities is 9.80 percent, whereas the subordinated notes have a cost of 10.61 percent (for simplicity here we ignore any differences in the duration and amortization profiles of the two bonds). This is calculated as:

$$(90\% \times 9.80\%) + (10\% \times 10.61\%) + 0.20\% = 10.08\%$$

This overall cost is lower than the target funding cost obtained from the balance sheet, which was 10.30 percent. This is the quantified benefit of the securitization process. Note that the funding cost obtained through securitization is lower than the yield on the loan book. Therefore, the original loan can be sold to the structure issuing the securities for a gain.

ABS STRUCTURES: A PRIMER ON PERFORMANCE METRICS AND TEST MEASURES

This section is an introduction to the performance measures on the underlying collateral of the ABS and MBS product. These would be of most interest to potential investors in ABS notes, but would also be noted by (amongst others) ratings agencies.

Collateral Types

ABS performance is largely dependent on consumer credit performance, so typical ABS structures include trigger mechanisms (to accelerate amortization) and reserve accounts (to cover interest shortfalls) to safeguard against poor portfolio performance. Though there is no basic difference in terms of the essential structure between CDO and ABS/MBS, some differences arise by the very nature of the collateral and the motives of the issuer. Interestingly, whereas a CDO portfolio may have 100–200 loans, ABS portfolios will often have thousands of obligors, in theory providing the necessary diversity in the pool of consumers.

We discuss briefly some prominent asset classes.

Auto Loans   Auto loan pools were some of the earliest to be securitized in the ABS market and still remain a major segment of the U.S. market. Investors traditionally have been attracted to the high asset quality involved and the fact that the vehicle offers an easily sellable, tangible asset in the case of obligor default. In addition, because a car is seen as an essential purchase and a short loan exposure (three to five years) provides a disincentive to refinance, no real prepayment culture exists. Prepayment speed is extremely stable and losses are relatively low, particularly in the prime sector.

Performance analysis:

- **Loss Curves** show expected cumulative loss through the life of a pool and so, when compared to actual losses, give a good measure of performance. In addition, the resulting loss forecasts can be useful to investors buying subordinate classes. Generally, prime obligors will have losses more evenly distributed, while nonprime and subprime lenders will have losses recognized earlier and so show a steeper curve. In both instances, losses typically decline in the latter years of the loan.
- The **Absolute Prepayment Speed** (also abbreviated as APS)[4] is a standard measure for prepayments, comparing actual period prepayments as a proportion to the whole pool balance. As with all prepayment metrics, this measure provides an indication of the expected maturity of the issued ABS and, essentially, the value of the call option on the issued ABS at any time.

Credit Cards   For specialized credit card banks, particularly in the United States, the ABS market has become the primary vehicle to fund increases in the volume of unsecured credit loans to consumers. Credit card pools are different from other types of ABSs in that loans have no predetermined term. A single obligor's credit card debt is often no more than six months, so the structure has to differ from other ABSs in that repayment speed needs to be controlled either through scheduled amortization or the inclusion of a

---

[4]First developed by Credit Suisse First Boston.

revolving period (where principal collections are used to purchase additional receivables).

Since 1991, the stand-alone trust has been replaced with a master trust as the preferred structuring vehicle for credit card ABS. The master trust structure allows an issuer to sell multiple issues from a single trust and from a single, albeit changing, pool of receivables. Each series can draw on the cash flows from the entire pool of securitized assets with income allocated to each pro rata based on the invested amount in the master trust.

Consider the example structure represented by Exhibit 1.3. An important feature is excess spread, reflecting the high yield on credit card debt. In addition, a financial guarantee is included as a form of credit enhancement, given the low rate of recoveries and the absence of security on the collateral. Excess spread released from the trust can be shared with other series suffering interest shortfalls.

EXHIBIT 1.3   Master trust structure

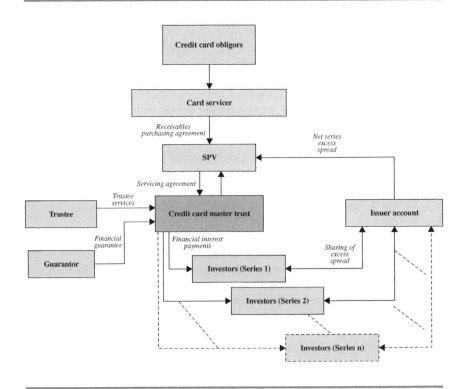

Performance analysis:

▪ The **Delinquency Ratio** is measured as the value of credit card receivables overdue for more than 90 days as a percentage of total credit card receivables. The ratio provides an early indication of the quality of the credit card portfolio.

▪ The **Default Ratio** refers to the total amount of credit card receivables written off during a period as a percentage of the total credit card receivables at the end of that period. Together, these two ratios provide an assessment of the credit loss on the pool and are normally tied to triggers for early amortization and so require reporting through the life of the transaction.

▪ The **Monthly Payment Rate (MPR)**[5] reflects the proportion of the principal and interest on the pool that is repaid in a particular period. The ratings agencies require every non-amortizing ABS to establish a minimum as an early-amortization trigger.

Mortgages   The MBS sector is notable for the diversity of mortgage pools that are offered to investors. Portfolios can offer varying duration as well as both fixed and floating debt. The most common structure for agency MBS is pass-through, where investors are simply purchasing a share in the cash flow of the underlying loans. Conversely, nonagency MBS (including CMBS), have a senior and a tranched subordinated class with principal losses absorbed in reverse order.

The other notable difference between RMBS and CMBS is that the CMBS is a nonrecourse loan to the issuer as it is fully secured by the underlying property asset. Consequently, the debt service coverage ratio (DSCR) becomes crucial to evaluating credit risk.

Performance analysis:

▪ **Debt Service Coverage Ratio (DSCR)** is given by net operating income/debt payments, and so indicates a borrower's ability to repay a loan. A DSCR of less than 1.0 means that there is insufficient cash flow generated by the property to cover required debt payments.

▪ The **Weighted Average Coupon (WAC)** is the weighted coupon of the pool, which is obtained by multiplying the mortgage rate on each loan by its balance. The WAC will therefore change as loans are repaid, but at any point in time, when compared to the net coupon payable to investors, it gives us an indication of the pool's ability to pay.

---

[5]This is not a prepayment measure because credit cards are non-amortizing assets.

▓ The **Weighted Average Maturity (WAM)** is the average weighted (weighted by loan balance) of the remaining terms to maturity (expressed in months) of the underlying pool of mortgage loans in the MBS. Longer securities are by nature more volatile, so a WAM calculated on the stated maturity date avoids the subjective call of whether the MBS will mature and recognizes the potential liquidity risk for each security in the portfolio. Conversely, a WAM calculated using the reset date will show the shortening effect of prepayments on the term of the loan.

The **Weighted Average Life (WAL)** of the notes at any point in time is

$$s = \sum t \cdot \mathrm{PF}(s)$$

where

$$\mathrm{PF}(s) = \text{Pool factor at } s$$
$$t = \text{Actual}/365$$

We illustrate this measure using the example shown in Exhibit 1.4.

It is the time-weighted maturity of the cash flows that allows potential investors to compare the MBS with other investments with similar maturity. These tests apply uniquely to MBS because principal is returned through the life of the investment on such transactions.

Forecasting prepayments is crucial to computing the cash flows of MBS. Though the underlying payment remains unchanged, prepayments, for a given price, reduce the yield on the MBS. There are a number of methods used to estimate prepayment; two commonly used ones are the constant prepayment rate (CPR) and the PSA method.

The CPR approach is:

$$\mathrm{CPR} = 1 - (1 - \mathrm{SMM})^{12}$$

where **Single Monthly Mortality (SMM)** is the single-month proportional prepayment.

An SMM of 0.65 percent means that approximately 0.65 percent of the remaining mortgage balance at the beginning of the month, less the scheduled principal payment, will prepay that month.

The CPR is based on the characteristics of the pool and the current expected economic environment, as it measures prepayment during a given month in relation to the outstanding pool balance.

The **Public Securities Association (PSA)** has a metric for projecting prepayment that incorporates the rise in prepayments as a pool seasons. A pool of mortgages is said to have 100 percent PSA if its CPR starts at 0 and increases by 0.2 percent each month until it reaches 6 percent in month 30. It is a constant 6 percent after that. Other prepayment scenarios can be

EXHIBIT 1.4 Sample weighted average life (WAL) calculation

IPD	Dates	Actual Days (a)	PF(t)	Principal Paid	O/S	a/365	PF(t)*(a/365)
0	21/11/2003	66	1.00		89,529,500.00	0.18082192	0.18082192
1	26/01/2004	91	0.94	5,058,824.00	84,470,588.00	0.24931507	0.23522739
2	26/04/2004	91	0.89	4,941,176.00	79,529,412.00	0.24931507	0.22146757
3	26/07/2004	91	0.83	4,823,529.00	74,705,882.00	0.24931507	0.20803536
4	25/10/2004	91	0.78	4,705,882.00	70,000,000.00	0.24931507	0.19493077
5	24/01/2005	91	0.73	4,588,235.00	65,411,765.00	0.24931507	0.18215380
6	25/04/2005	91	0.68	4,470,588.00	60,941,176.00	0.24931507	0.16970444
7	25/07/2005	91	0.63	4,352,941.00	56,588,235.00	0.24931507	0.15758269
8	24/10/2005	92	0.58	4,235,294.00	52,352,941.00	0.25205479	0.14739063
9	24/01/2006	90	0.54	4,117,647.00	48,235,294.00	0.24657534	0.13284598
10	24/04/2006	91	0.49	4,000,000.00	44,235,294.00	0.24931507	0.12318314
11	24/07/2006	92	0.45	3,882,353.00	40,352,941.00	0.25205479	0.11360671
12	24/10/2006	92	0.41	3,764,706.00	36,588,235.00	0.25205479	0.10300784
13	24/01/2007	90	0.37	3,647,059.00	32,941,176.00	0.24657534	0.09072408
14	24/04/2007	91	0.33	3,529,412.00	29,411,765.00	0.24931507	0.08190369
15	24/07/2007	92	0.29	3,411,765.00	26,000,000.00	0.25205479	0.07319849
16	24/10/2007	92	0.25	3,294,118.00	22,705,882.00	0.25205479	0.06392448
17	24/01/2008	91	0.22	3,176,471.00	19,529,412.00	0.24931507	0.05438405
18	24/04/2008	91	0.18	3,058,824.00	16,470,588.00	0.24931507	0.04586606
19	24/07/2008		-	16,470,588.00	-	WAL	2.57995911

specified as multiples of 100 percent PSA. This calculation helps derive an implied prepayment speed assuming mortgages prepay slower during their first 30 months of seasoning.

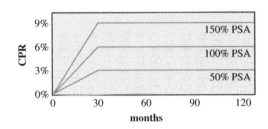

$$PSA = [CPR/(.2)(m)] * 100$$

where

$m =$ number of months since origination

Summary of Performance Metrics

Exhibit 1.5 lists the various performance measures we have introduced in this chapter, and the asset classes to which they apply.

SECURITIZATION: FEATURES OF THE 2007–2008 FINANCIAL CRISIS[6]

Following rapid growth in volumes during 2002–2006, during 2007 the securitization market came to a virtual standstill as a direct impact of the subprime mortgage default and the crash in asset-backed commercial paper trading. Investors lost confidence in a wide range of parameters. The liquidity crunch in money markets led to the credit crunch in the economy and worldwide recession. Globalization and integrated banking combined with the widespread investment in structured credit products to transmit the effects of U.S. mortgage defaults worldwide. A result of the now globalized nature of the financial market was that the securitization market, in the form of asset-backed securities such as collateralized debt obligations (CDOs), was a major contributor in transmitting and magnifying the impact of poor-quality loan origination in the U.S. mortgage market.

In light of the decline in securitization volumes since 2007, we consider the factors that contributed to the fall in confidence in the market.

---

[6]This section was coauthored with Gino Landuyt, YieldCurve.com.

EXHIBIT 1.5 Summary of ABS analysis and performance metrics

Performance Measure	Calculation	Typical Asset Class
Public Securities Association (PSA)	$PSA = [CPR/(.2) \text{ (months)}]*100$	Mortgages, home equity, student loans
Constant prepayment rate (CPR)	$1 - (1 - SMM)^{12}$	Mortgages, home equity, student loans
Single monthly mortality (SMM)	Prepayment / Outstanding pool balance	Mortgages, home equity, student loans
Weighted average life (WAL)	$\sum (a/365) \cdot PF(s)$ where $PF(s) =$	Mortgages
Weighted average maturity (WAM)	Weighted maturity of the pool	Mortgages
Weighted average coupon (WAC)	Weighted coupon of the pool	Mortgages
Debt service coverage ratio (DSCR)	Net operating income / Debt payments	Commercial mortgages
Monthly payment rate (MPR)	Collections / Outstanding pool balance	All non-amortizing asset classes
Default ratio	Defaults / Outstanding pool balance	Credit card
Delinquency ratio	Delinquents / Outstanding pool balance	Credit card
Absolute prepayment speed (APS)	Prepayments / Outstanding pool balance	Auto loans, truck loans
Loss curves	Show expected cumulative loss	Auto loans, truck loans

Impact of the Credit Crunch   The flexibility and wide application of the securitization technique, though advantageous to banks that employed it, also contributed to its misuse in the markets. By giving banks the ability to move assets off the balance sheet, ABS became a vehicle by which low-quality assets such as subprime mortgages could be sold on to investors who had little appreciation of the credit risk they were taking on.

1. The shadow banking system
   In a classic banking regime there is no detachment between the borrower and the lender. The bank does its own credit analysis, offers the loan to its client, and monitors the client over the life of the loan. In securitization, however, the link between the borrower and the bank is disconnected. The loan is packaged into different pieces and moved onto an unknown client base. As a consequence, there is less incentive for the arranger to be risk conscious.
   This becomes a potential negative issue when banks set up a parallel circuit, now termed the "shadow banking" system, where they are not bound by a regulatory regime that normal banks must adhere to. For instance, in a vanilla banking regime banks must keep a certain percentage of deposits against their loans, but this does not apply if they fund themselves via the commercial paper market, which is uninsured by a central bank's discount window.
   As a consequence, the shadow banks' major risk is when their commercial paper investors do not want to roll their investment anymore and leave the shadow bank with a funding problem. As a result, they might need to tap into the outstanding credit lines of regulated banks or sell their assets at fire sale prices. This is what happened in the asset-backed commercial paper (ABCP) crash in August 2007.

2. The amount of leverage
   The shadow banking system in the form of special investment vehicles (SIVs) was highly leveraged. Typically the leverage ratio was around 1:15, but in some cases, as the search for yield in a bull market of tightening credit spreads intensified, the leverage ratios for some SIVs reached 1:40 and even 1:50. To put this into perspective, the hedge fund Long Term Capital Management (LTCM) was running a leverage of 1:30 at the time of its demise and created significant disruption of the markets in 1998 all by itself. In effect, what happened in 2007–2008 was hundreds of LTCMs all failing, all of which used a higher leverage ratio and were all setting up the same trade.
   The leverage factor in some of the products reached very high levels. After CDOs, more leverage was sought with CDO^2, which were CDO structures investing in other CDOs. At the end of 2006, ABN AMRO

Bank introduced the ultimate leverage product by issuing the constant proportion debt obligation (CPDO). This product was based on the constant proportion participation investment (CPPI) technique, but did the exact opposite. In a CPPI, a leveraged position is dynamically managed, and if the net asset value (NAV) decreases the structure will deleverage. In the CPDO, one does the opposite and increases the leverage if the NAV decreases.

3. Lack of transparency

   Some of these products became extremely complex and started to look like a black box that was difficult to analyze by outside parties who sought to make an assessment on the value of the investment. For instance, the mark-to-market value was not only related to credit spread widening of the tranche, but also changes in correlation risk within the credit portfolio, which had different impacts on different tranches in the structure. As a matter of fact, default correlation is a statistic that cannot be observed in the market, so any pricing model that uses it as an input parameter is, to a certain extent, subjective.

4. Credit rating agencies (CRA)

   The CRAs publicized their rating methodologies, which had the cachet of statistical logic but were not understood by all investors; moreover, they were in hindsight overly optimistic in issuing ratings to certain deals in which the models used assumed that the likelihood of a significant correction in the housing market on an (inter)national scale was virtually zero. The favorable overall economic conditions and the continuous rise in home prices over the past decade provided near-term cover for the deterioration in lending standards and the potential ramifications of any significant decline in asset prices.[7]

5. Accounting and liquidity

   The liquidity of most of these assets was overestimated. As a consequence, investors believed that AAA-rated securitized paper would have the same liquidity as plain vanilla AAA-rated paper and could therefore be easily funded by highly liquid commercial paper. A huge carry trade of long-dated assets funded by short-term liabilities was built up, and once the first losses in the subprime market started to make an impact, SPVs had to start unwinding the paper. Fund managers realized that there was a liquidity premium linked to their assets that they had not taken into account.

   The mark-to-market accounting rules accelerated the problem by creating a downward spiral of asset values as the secondary market dried

---

[7]SIFMA, *Survey on Restoring Confidence in the Securitization Market*, December 2008.

up. Banks had to mark ABS assets at the market price, unconnected with the default performance of the underlying portfolios; however, in a flight-to-quality environment all structured credit products became impossible to trade in the secondary market and values were marked down almost daily, in some cases down to virtually zero. The accounting rules force banks to take artificial hits to their capital without taking into account the actual performance of the pool of loans.

As a result of the interaction of all the preceding factors, following the U.S. mortgage market fallout and general investor negative sentiment, the new-issue securitization market came to a virtual standstill. As a technique, though, it offers considerable value to banks and investors alike, and its intelligent use can assist in general economic development.

In-House Securitization Transactions

Following the July–August 2007 implosion of the asset-backed commercial paper market, investor interest in ABS product dried up virtually completely. The growing illiquidity in the interbank market, which resulted in even large AA-rated banks finding it difficult to raise funds for tenures longer than one month, became acute following the collapse of Lehman Brothers in September 2008. To assist banks in raising funds, central banks starting with the U.S. Federal Reserve and European Central Bank (ECB), and subsequently the Bank of England (BoE), relaxed the criteria under which they accepted collateral from banks to whom they were advancing liquidity. In summary, the central banks announced that asset-backed securities, including mort-gage-backed securities and other ABS, would now be eligible as collateral at the daily liquidity window.

As originally conceived, the purpose of these moves was to enable banks to raise funds from their respective central bank, using existing ABS on their balance sheet as collateral. Very quickly, however, the banks began to originate new securitization transactions, using illiquid assets held on their own balance sheet (such as residential mortgages or corporate loans) as collateral in the deal. The issued notes would be purchased by the bank itself, making the deal completely in-house. These new purchased ABS tranches would then be used as collateral at the central bank repo window.

This activity continued well beyond the period immediately after the 2008 crash and it is still common. In an effort to create assets that are eligible for use as collateral at central bank funding facilities, banks may elect to undertake an in-house securitization.

Structuring Considerations   Essentially, a central bank deal is like any other deal, except that there is no buyer for the notes. Of course the issued notes must be structured such that they are eligible as collateral at the central bank where they are intended to be placed as collateral. There are also haircut considerations and the opportunity to structure it without consideration for investors. To be eligible for repo at the ECB, for example, deals have to fulfill certain criteria. These include:

Minimum requirements
- Public rating of triple-A or higher at first issue.
- Only the senior tranche can be repoed.
- No exposure to synthetic securities. The ECB rules state that the cash flow in generating assets backing the asset-backed securities must not consist in whole or in part, actually or potentially, of credit-linked notes or similar claims resulting from the transfer of credit risk by means of credit derivatives. Therefore, the transaction should expressly exclude any types of synthetic assets or securities.
- Public presale or new issue report issued by the agency rating the facility, either listed in Europe (e.g., the Irish Stock Exchange) or with book entry capability in Europe (e.g., Euroclear, Clearstream).

Haircut considerations
- Collateralized loan obligation (CLO) securities denominated in euro will (taking effect from March 2009) incur a haircut of 12 percent regardless of maturity or coupon structure.
- For the purposes of valuation, in the absence of a trading price within the past five days, or if the price is unchanged over that period, a 5 percent valuation markdown is applied. This equates to an additional haircut of 4.4 percent.
- CLO securities denominated in USD will incur the usual haircuts but with an additional initial margin of between 10 percent and 20 percent to account for foreign exchange (FX) risk.

Other considerations
- Can incorporate a revolving period (external investors normally would not prefer this).
- Can be a simple two-tranche setup. The junior tranche can be unrated and subordinated to topping off the cash reserve.
- Off-market swap.
- One rating agency (the BoE requires two).
- There can be no in-house currency swap (this must be with an external counterparty).

The originator also must decide whether the transaction is to be structured to accommodate replenishment of the portfolio or whether the portfolio should be static. ECB transactions are clearly financing transactions for the bank and as such the bank will wish to retain flexibility to sell or refinance some or all of the portfolio at any time should more favorable financing terms become available to it. For this reason there is often no restriction on the ability to sell assets out of the portfolio, provided that the price received by the issuer is not less than the price paid by it for the asset (par), subject to adjustment for accrued interest. This feature maintains maximum refinancing flexibility and has been agreed to by the rating agencies in previous transactions.

Whether or not replenishment is incorporated into the transaction depends on a number of factors. If it is considered likely that assets will be transferred out of the portfolio (in order to be sold or refinanced), then replenishment enables the efficiency of the CDO structure to be maintained by adding new assets rather than running the existing transaction down and having to establish a new structure to finance additional or future assets. However, if replenishment is incorporated into the transaction, the rating agencies will have to carry out diligence on the bank to satisfy themselves on the capabilities of the bank to manage the portfolio. Also, the recovery rates assigned to a static portfolio will be higher than those assigned to a manager portfolio. The decision on whether to have a managed or static transaction will have an impact on the documentation for the transaction and the scope of the bank's obligations and representations.

Example of In-House Deal During 2007–2009 over 100 banks in the European Union undertook in-house securitizations in order to access the ECB discount window, as funding sources in the interbank market dried up.[8] A United Kingdom banking institution, the Nationwide Building Society, acquired an Irish banking entity during 2008 it was rumored solely in

---

[8]The entire business model of a large number of banks as well as shadow banks such as structured investment vehicles (SIVs) had depended on available liquidity from the interbank market, which was rolled over on a short-term basis such as weekly or monthly and used to fund long-dated assets such as RMBS securities that had much longer maturities and that themselves could not be realized in a liquid secondary market once the 2007 credit crunch took hold. This business model unraveled after the credit crunch, with its most notable casualties being Northern Rock PLC and the SIVs themselves, which collapsed virtually overnight. Regulatory authorities responded by requiring banks to take liquidity risk more seriously, with emphasis on longer-term average tenor of liabilities and greater diversity on funding sources (for example, see the UK FSA's CP 08/22 document at www.fsa.org). We discuss liquidity management in *Bank Asset and Liability Management* (John Wiley & Sons Limited, 2007) and *The Principles of Banking* (John Wiley & Sons Limited, 2012).

EXAMPLE 1.3: FASTNET SECURITIES 3 LIMITED

Fastnet Securities 3 Limited

Class	Balance	% of total	Rating (S&P)	WAL (years)	Legal final	Basis	Margin (bp)
A1	1,920,000,000	24%	AAA	2.91	Nov-2049	1-mo Euribor	40
A2	5,040,000,000	63%	AAA	3.15	Nov-2049	1-mo Euribor	45
B	1,040,000,000	13%	n/r	3.08	Nov-2049	1-mo Euribor	200
	8,000,000,000						
Cash reserve	400,000,000	5%					
Swap spread							150

Timing	
Cut-off date	12/5/2007
Final OC	12/17/2007
Settlement	12/17/2007
First payment date	2/11/2008

Key terms	
Issuer	Fastnet Securities 3 Ltd
Originator	Irish Life and Permanent
Sole arranger	Deutsche Bank AG
Trustee	Deutsche Trustee Company Ltd
First payment date	Monday, February 11, 2008
Day count	Actual/360
Listing	Irish Stock Exchange
Settlement	Euroclear/Clearstream
Legal maturity date	Thursday, November 11, 2049

Asset pool	
Mortgage pool	Residential mortgages originated by Irish Life in the Republic of Ireland
Number of obligors	35,672
Aggregate balance	EUR 8,319,049,200.22
Average balance	EUR 226,190
Largest mortgage	EUR 8,502,202
Weighted average Loan-to-Value Ratio (LTV)	83%
Weighted average seasoning	21 months
Weighted average remaining term	27.3 years
Longest maturity date	2-Nov-47

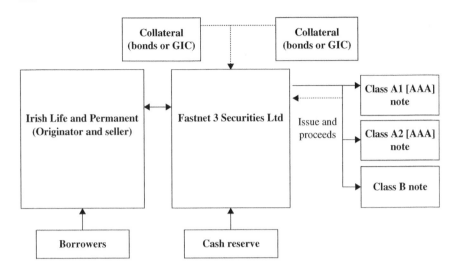

Note that this transaction was closed in December 2007, a time when the securitization market was essentially moribund in the wake of the credit crunch. An ABS note rated AAA could be expected to be marked to market at over 200 bps over LIBOR. Because the issued notes were purchased in entirety by the originator, who intended to use the senior tranche as collateral to raise funds at the ECB, the terms of the deal could be set at a purely nominal level; this explains the "40 bps over Euribor" coupon of the senior tranche.

order to access the ECB's discount window (a requirement for which was to have an office in the eurozone area).

One such public deal was Fastnet Securities 3 Limited, originated by Irish Life and Permanent PLC. Example 1.3 shows the deal highlights.

Market Yields and Prices Post Credit Crunch

During July and August 2009 a secondary market began to reemerge in European markets as investors began to pull back from the flight to quality exhibited during 2007–2008.

As an example of the yields that were trading during this time, see Exhibit 1.6. This shows the Bloomberg page DES for Columbus Nova, a CLO transaction closed in August 2006. At issue: The senior tranche of this deal, which was rated AAA, paid 26 bps over three-month LIBOR, and was priced at par. At the start of September 2009, the tranche was being offered at 87, over 400 bps over LIBOR. It was still rated AAA.

We consider postcrash developments in the market in Chapter 2.

EXHIBIT 1.6   Columbus Nova CLO DES page

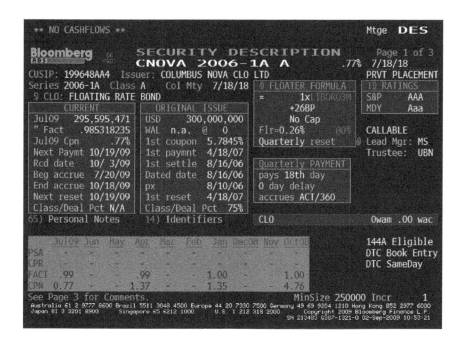

Source: Bloomberg LP. Reproduced with permission.

SUMMARY AND CONCLUSIONS

Securitization is a long-established technique that enables banks to manage their balance sheets with greater flexibility and precision. By employing it, a bank can work toward ensuring optimum treatment of its assets for funding, regulatory capital, and credit risk management purposes. In addition, in the postcrash era the securitization tool continues to be used to create tradable notes that can then be used as collateral at the central bank.

The primary driver behind the decision to securitize part of the asset side of the balance sheet is one or more of the following:

- Funding: Assets that are unrepo-able may be securitized, which enables the bank to fund them via the capital market, or by creating notes that can be used as collateral at the central bank.
- Regulatory capital: This is a rarer reason driving securitization in the postcrash, Basel III era, however it is still possible to structure a deal that

reduces regulatory capital requirement, principally if "significant risk transfer" has taken place.

■ Risk management: Assets on the balance sheet expose the originator to credit risk, and this can be managed (either reduced, removed, or hedged) via securitization.

A secondary driver is client demand: The process of securitization creates bonds that can be sold, and investor demand for a note of specified credit risk, liquidity, maturity, and underlying asset class may well cause a bond to be created, via securitization, to meet this specific investor requirement. Whether a transaction is demand driven or issuer driven, it will always be created to meet at least one of the preceding requirements.

The mechanics of closing a securitization deal, which we cover in detail in subsequent chapters, can take anything from a few months to up to a year or more. The most important parts of the process are the legal review and drafting of transaction documents, and the rating agency review. The involvement of third parties, such as lawyers, trustees, agency services providers, and the rating agencies, is the key driver behind the cost of closing a securitization deal, and these costs are covered either by the deal itself or directly by the originating institution.

A wide range of asset classes can be securitized, with the most common being residential mortgages and corporate loans. Other asset classes include auto loans and credit card receivables. When assessing the risk exposure and performance of different types of ABS, investors will consider the behaviors and characteristics of the specific type of underlying asset. Some performance metrics are of course common to all types of assets, such as delinquency rate or the percentage of nonperforming loans.

A type of securitization unknown before the 2008 crash but now common is the in-house transaction. In this process, the originating bank will undertake all the usual steps to structure the deal, but will buy the ABS notes itself. These notes, which would be rated by a rating agency in the normal way, are then available to the bank to use as collateral, either in a repo transaction or to place with the central bank. The deal has thereby transformed illiquid assets on the bank's balance sheet into liquid notes that can then be used to raise funding.

REFERENCES

Choudhry, M. 2007. *Bank Asset and Liability Management.* Singapore: John Wiley & Sons Limited.

Sundaresan, S. 1997. *Fixed Income Markets and Their Derivatives.* Cincinnati, OH: South-Western Press.

CHAPTER 2

The Securitization Market Post-2007

In Chapter 1 we described the impact of the 2007–2008 financial crash on the securitization market. A straight comparison will suffice to illustrate this impact; for example, in 2007 U.S. market public and Rule 144A ABS issuance amounted to $863 billion. In 2008 and 2009 the same asset issuance was $230 billion.[1] This is a tremendous decline; indeed, the majority of the issuance was under the Term Asset-Backed Loan Facility (TALF), a support program introduced by the U.S. government during the financial crisis of 2007–2008. What this statistic also tells us is that securitization remains a viable and valuable asset class for both originators and investors, given that issuance did not disappear completely. Therefore, in this section we look briefly at the market in the immediate postcrash era and also discuss salient features of interest to investors.

MARKET OBSERVATION

A standard feature during the recovery in an economic cycle is that risk aversion decreases once the worst of the recession is over. For example, during 2009, UK AAA-rated residential MBS spreads tightened over 300 bps and were trading at 180 bps over LIBOR. This is considerably below the yields seen only six months previously. Exhibit 2.1 shows UK residential mortgage-backed securitization (RMBS) spreads over alternative bank funding sources (straight bank debt rated AA and bank-covered bonds) for the period 2005–2009.

---

[1]Source: Thomson Financial Securities Data.

EXHIBIT 2.1   UK RMBS spreads over bank debt and covered bonds

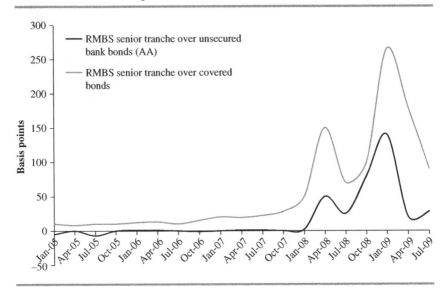

Source: Bloomberg L.P.

For other asset classes, the spreads came in by 2012. Exhibit 2.2 is the Bloomberg IYC page for housing asset class notes issued by U.S. government agencies. The curves are positively sloping with the U.S. Treasury curve, with spreads widening at longer maturities.[2]

The tranches of higher-quality underlying assets were trading at better spreads. On September 3, 2009, UK prime RMBS tranches were offered at prices still in the upper 90s, as shown in Exhibit 2.3a. Note, however, that the Granite issue, which was the vehicle of Northern Rock PLC, was being offered at a considerably lower price of €81.00.[3] All these are EUR-denominated securities. Contrast this with Exhibit 2.3b, which shows U.S. market commercial mortgage-backed securities (CMBS) yield spreads during August 2009. The commercial property sector in the United States was still suffering badly from the effects of the subprime fallout and the recession; consequently,

---

[2]Source: Bloomberg L.P.
[3]Northern Rock PLC, a commercial bank with its main business line in prime and subprime residential mortgages, suffered liquidity difficulties in August 2007 and was subsequently nationalized by the UK government.

EXHIBIT 2.2   Bloomberg page IYC for U.S. agency securities

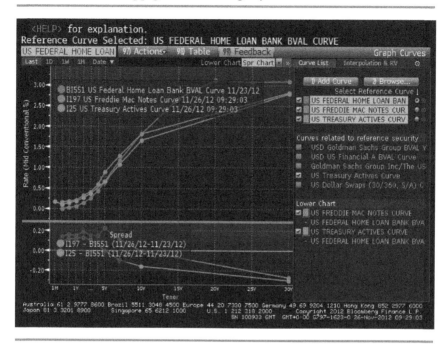

© Bloomberg L.P. Used with permission. Visit www.bloomberg.com.

even AAA-rated CMBS spreads remained high. In addition, USD-denominated securities generally paid a higher spread than EUR-denominated bonds of all classes.

In the postcrash market in the United States, the most common type of issuance was for auto-loan and credit card underlying. Exhibit 2.4 is a breakdown of ABS issuance in 2009. Note the virtual disappearance of the collateralized debt obligation (CDO) asset class. Exhibit 2.5 illustrates the impact on note spreads following the financial crisis.

Lower spreads provide a more feasible environment in which banks could start to reissue ABS again, as the cost of funding started to approach that of straight (unsecured) bank debt. As was the case prior to the crash, the economic rationale for banks to issue ABS over alternative sources of funding remains one of asset yield over liability yield. To make the case for ABS, banks must be able to place all tranches, and not just the AAA senior piece, into the market. In fact, under the postcrash regulatory regime, banks

EXHIBIT 2.3a Market-maker's offer page, UK RMBS senior tranches, September 2009

Name	Rating	Currency	Spread (bps)	Price	WAL (years)	Factor	Issuer
PERM 2006-1	AAA/Aaa	EUR	285	94.73	2.0	1.00	HBOS PLC
LOTHM 2006-1X	AAA/Aaa	EUR	190	97.64	1.3	0.91	Standard Life
HMI 2007-1	AAA/Aaa	EUR	190	97.15	1.6	1.00	Abbey National
HFP 9	AAA/Aaa	EUR	185	99.18	0.5	1.00	Abbey National
GMFM 2007-1X	AAA/Aaa	EUR	190	95.90	2.3	1.00	Barclays Bank
ARKLE 2006-1X	AAA/Aaa	EUR	190	95.36	2.6	1.00	Lloyds TSB
GRANM 2005-2	AAA/Aaa	EUR		81.00		0.63	Northern Rock

Source: Royal Bank of Scotland.

EXHIBIT 2.3b U.S. CMBS spreads to one-month LIBOR, August 2009

Tranche	Spread
AAA	1325
AA	3250
A	4250
BBB	5400
[1-mo LIBOR 0.3%]	

Source: Deutsche Bank.

EXHIBIT 2.4 U.S. ABS sector breakdown, 2009

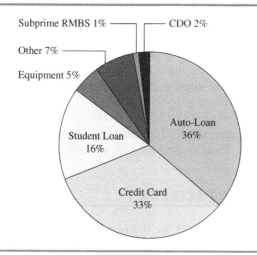

Source: Thomson Financial Securities Data.

EXHIBIT 2.5 U.S. floating-rate spreads, 2009

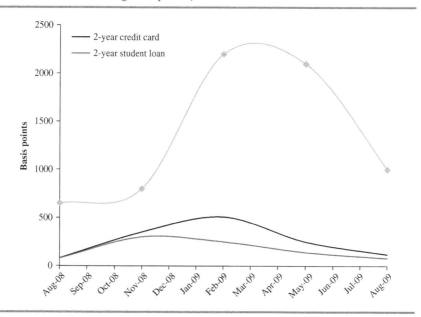

Source: Bloomberg L.P. (yield).

will need to do this if they are to secure any regulatory capital relief as a result of the deal (that is, they need to have transferred the entire credit risk to a third party).

During 2009, many bank assets (such as mortgages and student loans) did not yield sufficient margin to support a full capital structure ABS issue. Of course, a bank may wish to close a deal for other, more strategic reasons, such as encouraging investor interest and helping to reenergize the market, or to create collateral for posting at the central bank. A prime attraction, as was always the case, is that an ABS deal also diversifies funding sources for a bank, which is a key requirement of bank regulators such as the UK's Financial Services Authority (FSA) in the post-Lehman era.

IMPACT ON RATING AGENCIES

The status and reputation of the three main credit rating agencies (CRAs) suffered grievously in the wake of the 2007–2008 financial crisis. This issue caused many former ABS investors to refrain from reentering the market. As a result, the agencies reviewed their rating methodologies and criteria, as well as their base case assumptions. Chapter 4 looks in detail at Moody's methodology for ABS and CDO products, and we also review their main ratings checklist process that ABS originators need to follow ahead of the ratings review. The immediate impact of the review process was that the CRAs revised their performance and loss assumptions to take into account actual losses that occurred in the recession. The CRAs also took steps to publish more transparent disclosures as part of their ratings process.

The stability of credit ratings was most heavily damaged in the mortgage market sector. Investors in subprime and prime RMBS, CMBS, and CDOs of ABS (in which the underlying included MBS) observed the greatest deterioration in ratings during 2008–2009. CRAs publish ratings transition tables detailing the percentage of securities that were still the same rating after one year (or longer). Moody's also publishes downgrade rates, which are defined as the number of securities downgraded divided by the total number of outstanding securities at the beginning of the observation period.

In a report from 2009, Moody's reported that 7.38 percent of all the structured finance securities that it rated were downgraded in the period 1999–2008. This is a surprisingly low figure. If CDOs of ABS, home equity ABS, and RMBS are excluded, the figure is 3.18 percent.[4] For 2008 only,

---

[4]See Moody's Investors Service, *Structured Finance Rating Transitions: 1983–2008*, Special Report, March 2009.

however, the downgrade rate was 35.5 percent, and 12.1 percent when mortgage-related securities are excluded.

In response to the crisis and criticism of their methodology, the CRAs modified their approach. The definition of a rating itself did not change, but certain underlying assumptions were changed to reflect the observations from 2007–2008. In addition, CRAs undertook to provide greater transparency and disclosures as part of the ratings process.

One significant change that was adopted was that the ratings process now considers the liquidity and funding scenario for the originating or sponsoring entity: This had not been reviewed prior to the crash. The impact of this change is material, because the CRAs now take into account the liquidity position of the originator. Sponsors that are overly reliant on the ABS market, or have few alternative sources for their funding, are required to provide a higher level of credit enhancements for the structure. In some cases, the top AAA/Aaa rating is not available to such sponsors.

Following is a summary comparison of the new approaches of each of the three main CRAs.

Moody's Investors Service

According to its web site, a Moody's rating is a qualitative description of a quantitative measure of relative creditworthiness of a security. It is a forward-looking, 12-month risk assessment. The analysis undertaken to arrive at a rating is both qualitative and quantitative, although for a structured finance security the qualitative review is limited in comparison. The rating itself represents a probability of the likelihood of a security making full and timely payment of its principal and interest liabilities.

Moody's rating approach is essentially unchanged from its precrisis model, but has been modified in certain aspects of its detail. Greater weight is now given to operational features of the structure, the relationship of the structure with the sponsor, and the sponsor's access to alternative sources of liquidity. Based on this approach, some asset-class ABS products are now no longer assigned an Aaa rating, irrespective of the amount of credit enhancement that is built into the vehicle; this has been observed, for example, with specific types of auto ABS securities, as well as certain credit card issuers and equipment lease deals.[5]

---

[5]Some of the so-called credit card banks had relied excessively on the securitization market to raise finances and grow their balance sheet. For such firms, the lack of alternative sources of finance means that their ABS product is now unlikely to be assigned an Aaa rating unless the sponsor arranges for funding diversity.

Included in the new Moody's approach is the provision of V-scores and parameter sensitivities in its ratings report. The V-score is a measure of the potential variability of the inputs to the ratings process, and is designed to highlight the risk of such fluctuations to investors. Parameter sensitivities are a sensitivity analysis of these rating inputs.

Standard & Poor's

An S&P rating is also a qualitative measure of relative creditworthiness of a security within the rated population; however, it is also a measure specifically of the probability of default. The S&P review process also includes payment priority, recovery rate, and credit stability. Since the 2007 crisis, S&P has emphasized that its ratings are comparable across security type and asset class, and that they represent an ability to withstand specific macroeconomic scenarios. An AAA-rated bond in theory would not default in an economic scenario similar to the 1930s depression, whereas a BBB-rated bond would survive an equity market fall of 50 percent and unemployment rate of 10 percent (statistics that are similar to those observed in the 2007–2008 crash).

Fitch

Similar to the other CRAs, a Fitch rating is a measure of relative creditworthiness, with an emphasis (as with S&P) on probability of default. Fitch has also adopted a similar approach to Moody's in taking into account the liquidity and funding position of an originating entity when assigning the rating.

Alone among the CRAs, Fitch publishes an outlook for each rating, which is a medium-term view of rating stability alongside the 12-month formal rating. Two additional measures introduced by Fitch are loss severity ratings and recovery ratings. Loss severity ratings measure the adequacy of the size of the tranche under specified loss scenarios. The recovery rating is a measure of recovery value. Also unique to Fitch was the decision not to award the highest AAA rating to transactions that were deemed to be market value deals, which, broadly speaking, are those whose performance is linked to an external index or the trading value of underlying assets.

SUMMARY AND CONCLUSIONS

The securitization market remains a valuable tool for banks to use as part of their balance sheet management. The key focus for originators remains that of sourcing assets of sufficient credit quality and performance when transacting a deal, to ensure that investor requirements can be satisfied. That there remains demand, at lower levels, for ABS products speaks to the continuing needs of certain classes of investor for the risk-reward profiles of such notes.

The rating agencies' methodology for rating ABS notes takes into account lessons learned after the 2008 financial crash, and as a result certain of the more exotic underlying asset classes are rarely observed in the market. Also, market value type transactions are no longer able to obtain the highest AAA rating.

Two

Guide to Closing a Securitization Transaction

Part Two goes step by step through the procedure undertaken when designing and closing a securitization deal. The template description given in Chapters 3 and 4 applies to cash transactions in asset-backed securities, mortgage-backed securities, and corporate loan deals. However, they are applicable in principle to virtually any securitization structure and are intended to act as a project management checklist for practitioners.

The guidelines we provide here are brought to life in Part Three of the book, which looks at an actual transaction closed in 2009 and provides templates and illustrations that can be used by practitioners involved in other corporate loan and ABS transactions.

Chapter 5 illustrates a cash flow waterfall model. A defining element of a securitization deal is the liability notes tranching, which produces a waterfall of the order or priority of payments for investors and third parties to the deal. The model guidelines provided in Chapter 5 can be applied in most situations.

CHAPTER 3

Structuring and Execution of a Transaction

In this chapter we provide a checklist-style guide on the process, from start to finish, behind structuring a securitization deal. This process is complex and involves a number of parties, both internally (within the originating institution) and also externally (from service and other providers). The originator needs to undertake the steps described next as part of closing the deal, although not all of them will be applicable to the same degree.

Separate from the process described here, but running in parallel, is the legal review and the credit rating agency review, which we describe in the next chapter.

A SECURITIZATION PROCESS

The exercise of arranging a securitization transaction is in many ways one of project management. The process itself has some tasks that can run concurrently but also a number that are contingent on other outcomes. As with many projects, the path is not a consistent one; however, we show here a generic template for the order of the process followed in order to establish a transaction ready to bring to market.

Select Arranger

The task line (illustrated graphically in the generic time chart shown at each step we describe) begins with the formal appointment of an arranger. It is probably appropriate to mention there is a great deal of work required to put yourself in a position to win a mandate. Arranger banks maintain close relationships with other financial institutions, providing continual advice and market color on asset and liability strategies. It is hoped that this work will culminate with an offer from the issuer who, once having decided they would like to access the market, will invite their relationship banks to pitch for the transaction by way of a request for proposal (RFP). The RFP is similar to a corporate procurement process where bidders are asked to set out their credentials, assumptions, and pricing. Although this is quite a formulaic process, a successful bidder will still need to demonstrate its capability to provide for a smooth execution.

In reality, the RFP is opportunity to monetize what has, at times, been significant effort from a relationship perspective, and the proposal will require considerable research and analysis. A successful proposal will typically outline the depth of expertise and experience in the transaction team; an update on recent market events; and an understanding of the asset class, particularly in the context of the issuer's portfolio and motivations. Aside from issuer-led RFPs, a structuring bank can provide significantly more value-added where it can offer a securitization solution that encumbers an unusual asset class that is otherwise difficult to liquidate, repo, or transfer risk for, or is in a problematic jurisdiction.

Asset Analysis

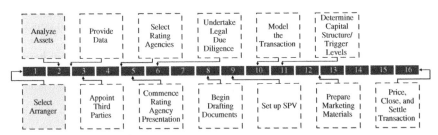

Later in this book we discuss data requirements for credit rating agency models, but ahead of such an exercise the arranger will want to do some preliminary analysis to get a good understanding of the portfolio to be securitized. This will mean requesting from the issuer a snapshot of the loan data (in whatever format they have) and discussions with relevant teams and personnel to better understand the characteristics of the underlying product.

The purpose of the analysis is to flush out any key issues that could either make a transaction problematic or create a need for additional structure features. Set out next are some of the various discussion points that could arise from an initial assessment.

Does the deal "wash its face"? Or is there sufficient yield on the assets to cover liabilities issued at a price that will be compelling in today's market? Securitization is the monetization of a portfolio of assets; specifically, future cash flows from those assets through the issuance of secured liabilities. It therefore stands to reason that the most rudimentary test is one of debt serviceability.

The asset yield to take into account here is the net yield that the securitization vehicle would yield once all expenses and exclusions are accounted for. This requires quantifying the level of expenses an issuer will need to bear for the transaction (key costs here would be portfolio servicing arrangements and any senior hedging transactions that would be required) but also understanding the nature of the gross yield figure provided by the portfolio seller.

Some portfolios have a "headline" yield figure for each loan, which cannot be taken at face value because they are either each subject to change during the loan period, or include payments that are related to other borrower costs that do not specifically relate to the loan to be securitized. One example of this could be the seller providing loan insurance to the borrower and embedding the corresponding premium in the chargeable rate to the borrower. It is important to understand the true composition of the yield number and any potential threats to the stability of that number.

The second limb to be considered is that of the pricing for the liabilities. Given that these are asset backed, all things being equal (that is, in a single-tranche, pass-through structure), the weighted average life of the assets would be equal to the weighted average life of the liabilities. Given the condition that investors will want a greater payoff for longer-dated maturities, there has to be some assessment of the yield in the context of the liabilities' weighted average life.

In reality there can be some manipulation of the liability maturity. A period of asset reinvestment can be used to extend the weighted average life of the bonds. This reinvestment feature is referred to as a *revolving period* and is where principal redemptions on assets are not used to pay down principal on the liabilities, but rather used to purchase further assets with similar characteristics from the issuer. This has the effect of delaying the amortization of the issued liabilities and so extending their scheduled tenor by the length of the revolving period.

Can we extract more juice? Or is there scope to create additional leverage in the structure? If the asset-to-liability equation is not satisfied, a less used but equally effective option is to extract greater available excess spread from the portfolio. We use the term less used because although there is more than one way to create leverage in the structure, it invariably comes at a cost to the equity holder, either in the way of potential reduced return or increased risk.

A tranched capital structure in itself creates some leverage for senior tranches, as interest amounts collected from the entire asset base are first used to cover the coupon for the senior liability only (which is a smaller comparative notional). Consequently, where additional spread is needed to service the senior notes (or even service the notes under credit rating agency stresses), the capital structure could feature an unrated junior note that is retained by the originator.

The simple approach would be for this unrated junior note to have an unusually low coupon—lower than the coupons for more senior, less risky liabilities in the capital structure. Holding such a note, however, can create accounting problems for some originators, as retained notes to be held at par (for accounting purposes) need to demonstrate market level coupons. This can be mitigated by assigning the junior note a par value coupon where nonpayment of interest due to insufficient funds causes nothing more than a deferral until the following payment date.

Many transactions feature reserves, which provide additional credit enhancement to structures and are funded through subordinated loans provided by the originator. Such subordinated loan agreements could be structured to provide the originator with the flexibility to provide further drawdown loans to the issuer (in effect cash injections) at their discretion. What is important to remember here is that where subordinated loans provided by the originator are contingent on some event occurring, an investor cannot rely on these amounts at rating levels above that of the entity providing the subordinated loan.

An originator artificially increasing the amount of spread available to a transaction is not unheard of and was often used for transactions that were put together post-2008 as originators tried to optimize the size of European Central Bank–eligible senior tranches in open market operations. In these in-house transactions, a more common mechanism was for the originator to act as swap counterparty and enter into off-market hedges that would be struck in the favor of the issuer. A simple example would be the issuer paying to the swap counterparty all interest amounts from a portfolio and receiving a fixed amount that would be greater than the weighted average coupon from the portfolio (effectively providing a raised floor).

We do not outline all the potential approaches to optimizing or maximizing the amount of interest available for a structure to pay down specific liabilities because of the large variety of options that can be considered. Those already mentioned are the most typical in the context of public or rated securitizations. If a credit rating agency is not involved, there is even more scope for creativity. One such example could be to broaden the scope of authorized investments that amounts in the issuer accounts could be used toward. This could be as simple as lower-rated, higher-yielding assets or as complicated as purchasing put options where the downside would be limited to the cost of the premium but the upside could be considerable. These would be in the context of investment in indices that could be tied to the return of specific subordinated tranches. Such transactions, however, would be a movement away from securitization and more toward a wider credit structured solution.

Can we obtain the assets when we need to? Otherwise, what is the effectiveness of the security package that noteholders have recourse to? Fundamental to securitization is that the assets sold to the issuing vehicle are ring-fenced from the bankruptcy estate of the seller. Aside from unsecured consumer loans, a transfer of secured assets requires in each instance the transfer of the mortgage (i.e., the right to enforce on the tangible asset) in addition to the loan itself. In most jurisdictions, a transfer of the loan effects a transfer of the corresponding mortgage also, but this is not always the case (shipping loans being an obvious example, where the mortgage is governed by the law of the ship flag).

An arranging bank will analyze any potential obstacles in transferring to, and ring-fencing assets with, a special purpose vehicle. Some jurisdictions are more problematic with respect to free transfer of assets or data. For example, in Poland, the Personal Data Act prohibits the disclosure of personal data other than with the debtor's consent. Given that most portfolios run into the tens of thousands of loans, this creates an insurmountable logistical nightmare. It is one reason why Polish MBS deals have never been put together. True sale securitization in Poland can be carried out in line with the Act on Investment Funds by way of sub-participation. Under a sub-participation, the purchase price is recognized up front, but the costs are amortized over time, which creates a large tax liability at the moment of sale.

Additionally, some thought has to be given to how secured creditors could liquidate if necessary, and if there would be any threats or additional expenses incurred in doing so. This will also vary considerably between legal jurisdictions and across asset classes. Consider the following:

- Auto loans—if the issuer becomes lender of record for the cars themselves, does it then become responsible for taxes on the vehicle and fines incurred by the obligor?
- Shipping loans—if the issuer takes ownership of the ship, does it then also become responsible for maintenance of the ship, payment of crew salaries, and so forth?

There are a number of risks to the assets themselves that need to be evaluated. Are they subject to some form of regulatory or legal control that could impinge on their subsequent value? Could technological advancements render them obsolete, or would there be reputational concerns in liquidating the portfolio (if loans are secured against consumer goods, it would be practically impossible to enter into someone's home and retrieve them)?

To summarize, the viability of a trade from a security perspective considers the likelihood of transferring and ultimately securing assets on behalf of the secured creditor. Part of the portfolio analysis will also consider the cost of holding or liquidating (haircut) such assets if and when the issuer would be required to do so.

Provide Data

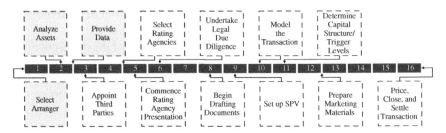

As mentioned previously, for an initial asset analysis, the issuer will be asked to produce the data in a format that they have on hand. As part of a rating process, the credit rating agencies have specific data requirements for the issuer. In instances where an external rating is not sought (some asset finance trades, for example), investors will often have their own internal rating approach that will utilize credit rating agency models. Consequently, the data demands from the issuer will largely be the same.

The provision of data, particularly for first-time issuers, is one of the more onerous aspects of the process. For an arranger, this often means working closely with the issuer's IT department. At the extremes, this phase can take up to six months.

Loan-Level Data   Specific loan-by-loan information requirements will vary depending on each asset class. The credit rating agencies will typically provide a minimum set of characteristics that will need information on an individual level. This information includes all pertinent commercial points of the underlying loan, such as balance outstanding, interest rate, and currency, together with relevant information on the borrower, including parameters pertinent to the originator's credit assessment or risk grading of that borrower. For secured portfolios, asset information will also be included.

The originator will provide several versions of this file throughout the process, particularly as the structuring process crosses payment cycles. Examples are provided in Exhibits 3.1 and 3.2. Additionally, this information needs

EXHIBIT 3.1 File snapshot: loan level data

Loan ID	Currency	Original balance	Current balance	Appraisal value	LTV	Type of rate	Interest rate	Original term	Remaining term
001	EUR	168,000	120,000	225,000	53%	Fixed	5.25	29	344
002	EUR	28,800	128,498	188,500	68%	Fixed	7.25	25	268
003	EUR	72,600	172,600	72,800	237%	Fixed	3.50	30	360
004	EUR	125,000	116,611	117,000	100%	Fixed	6.75	30	254
005	EUR	58,800	258,729	359,000	72%	Fixed	5.75	31	359
006	EUR	57,722	57,722	58,000	100%	Fixed	6.00	31	359

EXHIBIT 3.2 Stratification table by interest rate

Interest rate (%)	Current balance	Current balance	Number of loans	% of loans
1.75–3.24	243,750	0.06	3	0.09
3.25–4.74	21,014,868	4.97	150	4.30
4.75–6.24	147,802,964	34.96	800	22.94
6.25–7.74	240,341,940	56.85	2,300	65.94
7.75–9.24	12,222,328	2.89	200	5.73
> 9.25 =	1,117,712	0.26	35	1.00
Total:	422,743,562	100	3,488	100

Minimum: 1.75
Maximum: 10.00
Average: 6.00

to be provided on an ongoing basis to the credit rating agencies as part of their rating surveillance. For more established asset classes such as mortgages (residential, nonconforming, and commercial), where there have been a large number of deals rated, rating agencies may provide templates for originators to complete. It is in the originator's interest to provide as much information as possible. For corporate portfolios, originators are asked for information at both the obligor and obligor group level.

If an obligor has a single loan that is collateralized by more than one piece of the collateral, then details need to be given on each. Similarly, if a single piece of collateral provides security for more than one loan, then a breakout of each of those loans is required. In this instance, simply aggregating the loan balances is insufficient, as each of those single loans may have been offered at different terms and with different maturities, depending on obligor behavior. An additional layer of complexity is introduced if a single item of collateral services loans from different obligors or obligor groups. An example of this could be a single asset, such as a ship, providing the collateral for a loan that has been sub-participated out to more than one lender. There are several permutations that could arise here, but the overriding objective is to ensure there is total transparency of the size and nature of exposures that are being securitized, and the relationship between default on a single exposure and the subsequent claim over the collateral.

For less granular, corporate portfolios where an actuarial approach cannot be applied, rating agencies will look to assign a unique default probability to each underlying obligor and as such, the originator is expect to provide for each credit either a rating (either public or shadow rating) or an internal credit score. In instances where an internal credit score is provided, the rating agency will undertake a due diligence of the scoring system applied for the portfolio.

It is important to note that the rating agencies recognize some off-the-shelf risk-scoring products. Originators that use such models and can demonstrate they have been used to score obligors in the pool are given credit for doing so.

Historical Data For most loan portfolios, the originator is required to produce historical data going back at least three years (and ideally beyond that to five years or more), as follows:

- The evolution of the portfolio with dynamic month-end balances and historical yields.
- Historical levels of prepayments—best demonstrated by the amount of loans prepaying each month on a dynamic basis.
- Portfolio delinquencies on a dynamic basis, broken out by monthly delinquency buckets.
- Portfolio defaults on a static (vintage) basis. By vintage, we mean to demonstrate the evolution of the occurrence of defaults for each specific cohort. In Exhibit 3.3 we are looking in the first line only at those loans originated in 2006 Q4 and the size and speed of default accumulation. Similarly, line 2 covers only the performance of the 2007 Q1 vintage. Each subsequent line provides us one less data point, which provides for the diminishing nature of the loans in the table. The vintage analysis shows us outlying vintages in terms of performance (which can be attributed to changes in servicing procedures or market conditions) and also gives an expectation of peak levels of default, which are evidenced by a flattening effect of the curve.
- Portfolio recoveries on a static (vintage) basis. Similar to defaults, with the distinction that the data is to show the amount of assets defaulted in a given month and the subsequent size and timing of recoveries on those assets. Again, there is an expectation of recovery levels to be inferred here. The agency may only give credits to recoveries up to a certain period in time and this interval will almost certainly be capped by the time between the longest-dated loan in the portfolio (or possible under the loan criteria) and the legal final maturity of the issued liabilities.

The preceding data requirements are a minimum only. There will probably be requests for more information on borrower circumstances (employment, marital status, age, etc.) and origination channels for the loans. Should there be evidence of a correlation between certain loan or borrower characteristics and performance, it may be possible (given sufficient

EXHIBIT 3.3 Portfolio defaults, historic basis

Percentage Defaulted	1	2	3	4	5	6	7	8	9	10	11	12	13	14	15	16	17	18
2006/Q4	0.00%	0.00%	0.00%	0.10%	0.25%	0.68%	1.61%	3.06%	4.98%	5.48%	6.46%	7.94%	8.94%	9.20%	9.50%	9.80%	10.00%	10.10%
2007/Q1	0.00%	0.00%	0.00%	0.06%	0.24%	0.83%	1.83%	3.25%	3.87%	4.97%	6.50%	8.57%	8.85%	9.40%	9.70%	10.20%	10.40%	
2007/Q2	0.00%	0.00%	0.00%	0.04%	0.32%	0.90%	2.00%	2.45%	3.32%	4.60%	5.30%	6.69%	7.70%	8.60%	9.38%	9.70%		
2007/Q3	0.00%	0.00%	0.00%	0.07%	0.46%	1.25%	1.73%	2.66%	4.09%	5.99%	6.49%	7.34%	8.51%	10.01%	10.26%			
2007/Q4	0.00%	0.00%	0.00%	0.11%	0.51%	0.99%	2.00%	3.62%	5.79%	6.31%	7.18%	8.45%	10.04%	10.38%				
2008/Q1	0.00%	0.00%	0.00%	0.09%	0.51%	1.44%	2.93%	4.00%	5.62%	6.66%	8.16%	9.10%	9.70%					
2008/Q2	0.00%	0.00%	0.00%	0.06%	0.53%	1.58%	3.27%	3.98%	5.25%	7.01%	8.30%	9.00%						
2008/Q3	0.00%	0.00%	0.00%	0.14%	1.00%	3.70%	5.50%	7.00%	8.70%	9.70%	10.50%							
2008/Q4	0.00%	0.00%	0.00%	0.10%	1.20%	3.50%	5.00%	7.30%	8.40%	9.20%								
2009/Q1	0.00%	0.00%	0.00%	0.13%	0.90%	1.76%	3.00%	5.20%	6.40%									
2009/Q2	0.00%	0.00%	0.00%	0.11%	0.67%	1.86%	3.20%	4.69%										
2009/Q3	0.00%	0.00%	0.01%	0.12%	0.83%	1.50%	3.25%											
2009/Q4	0.00%	0.00%	0.00%	0.14%	0.75%	1.63%												
2010/Q1	0.00%	0.00%	0.00%	0.06%	0.58%													
2010/Q2	0.00%	0.00%	0.00%	0.08%														
2010/Q3	0.00%	0.00%	0.00%															
2010/Q4	0.00%	0.00%																
2011/Q1	0.00%																	

information) for the agency to formulate assumptions accordingly. If, for example, there was evidence that portfolio performance was being dragged down by the performance of, say, loans originating from a particular channel, limiting their percentage featuring in the portfolio could provide for better overall base case scenarios for the transaction.

Credit rating agencies will rely on this data, together with data points they already have on the asset class and jurisdiction of the transaction, in order to form a base case view of expected performance. Post-2008 crisis, the quantity of data required is more onerous, particularly in peripheral jurisdictions. Where agencies have felt they cannot formulate reasonable assumptions, they will not rate the transaction. Such instances could include available data (from originator or otherwise) not covering the average life of the assets or vintage curves showing no evidence of peaking.

Exhibits 3.4 and 3.5 are examples of two different sets of vintage curves.

Exhibit 3.4 shows the levels of incremental defaults to be diminishing, and the flattening effect produced by the curves allows us to infer that cumulative defaults tend to peak at around the 10 percent level.

Exhibit 3.5 leads us to a different conclusion. Default levels are following the same broad trends, but are not showing any signs of abating. From this, it is difficult to form a firm view on where defaults will ultimately peak.

EXHIBIT 3.4   Default vintage curves I

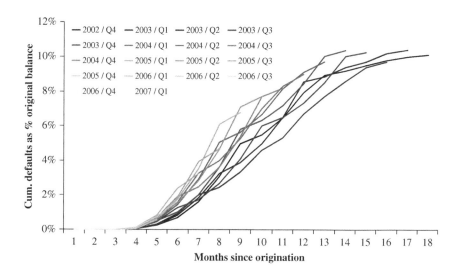

EXHIBIT 3.5   Default vintage curves II

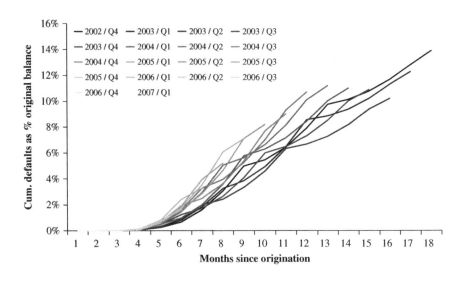

For corporate loan portfolios in CLO transactions, vintage default and recovery information will need to be supplemented with internal information on migration history. Rating agencies have published credit curves based on historic observed defaults—giving the probability of default (PD) at each rating level over a number of years. These curves will be calibrated for each portfolio given the information provided.

Appoint Third Parties

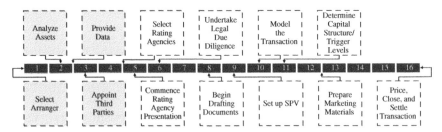

The arranger is responsible for ensuring the appropriate third parties are in place for the transaction. The costs for mandating such parties is borne by the issuer or sponsor, so often these roles are put out to tender through an RFP process. It is also important to note that the point in the process where such parties are introduced is also relevant. Legal counsels are integral to the documentation process and any fundamental legal obstacles to a transaction need to be addressed as soon as practically possible. That said, law firms often give fee quotes that rely on assumptions for the time the transaction will take to complete. Bringing a law firm before the originator has some certainty that data will be available will lead to unnecessary charges being incurred if fee cap assumptions are breached. In contrast, bringing too many parties into the transaction—particularly while the structure is being developed (and so continually being modified) can provide for an inefficient process.

Some of the key third party roles are set out next, together with some considerations the arranger may have when making recommendations to the sponsor.

Trustee   A trustee would be appointed to administer the duties of the special purpose vehicle (SPV) for the life of the transaction, while at all times protecting the interests of the transaction noteholders. Throughout the structuring process, the trustee will work, primarily with the arranger, to ensure that the SPV has received clear title to the assets, that the security interests are perfected, and that the SPV is bankruptcy remote. The trustee will monitor the compliance of other parties to their respective duties set out in the transaction documents and in particular that the originator is abiding by its respective obligations with respect to the asset portfolio. In the main, these roles are largely passive, in that the trustee is often notified of breaches of trust and then notifies all relevant parties accordingly.

Leading trust providers in the market have sought market share with enhanced reporting capabilities and offering clients a "one-stop shop" for all fiduciary and agency roles in a transaction. Historically, this provided for a market where mandating the trustee was driven largely by a combination of pricing and quality of service and reporting. From an arranger's perspective, a trustee serving as an efficient partner in the documentation review process would be as much of a deciding factor as anything else. During and since the 2008 crisis, however, where the trustee was called on to take a more active role in transactions, trust shops have begun to differentiate themselves from each other with respect to their approaches to *inter alia* exercising discretionary judgment and obtaining noteholder consent.

As mentioned, trustees are allowed to *inter alia* modify documentation terms, waive minor breaches, and correct manifest errors—in all cases where it is deemed to be in the interest of noteholders. From an arranger's perspective, there was, during the financial crisis, frustration dealing with trust players who were perceived to be overly risk averse and who insisted on seeking noteholder consent where it was known other trust shops were taking a more proactive approach on similar issues.

To highlight one such example, as liquidity providers came under rating downgrade pressure there was focus on a number of outstanding transactions where the downgrade triggers set at issuance were more conservative than required under the agencies' more recent criteria. Liquidity providers (who often acted as arranger in those transactions) were of the view that bringing trigger language in line with current criteria would not adversely affect transaction ratings but would also be to the benefit of noteholders. A liquidity provider entering into a transaction before the onset of the crisis would have done so at relatively low cost to the issuer. Should a liquidity provider—who was prepared to continue providing liquidity—need to be replaced, it would be almost certain that the replacement provider would charge a significantly higher commitment fee in what was a distressed environment. In effect, the issuer would be incurring greater cost as a consequence of an event that was not adversely affecting note ratings.

Considering also that the consent process incurs cost, takes time (a minimum of 21 days to hold a noteholder meeting) and more often than not fails to be passed due to noteholder apathy, going forward there is now greater scrutiny on the position of the trustee on such issues. Arrangers now give greater weight to resourcing and experience when mandating the trustee.

In the current market there has been some discussion on the role of a super trustee—in effect, a trustee with a greater role and wider responsibilities —but this has yet to take off in securitization transactions.

Cash Manager   The responsibility of the cash manager in a securitization is to manage the cash of the issuing vehicle, and to do so in accordance with the guidelines set out under the transaction documents. In effect this is a responsibility for all liability-side calculations in the structure and the disbursement of cash on each and every payment date.

The cash manager will take the information provided by the servicer in its servicer report in order to determine the amounts that will be available to the issuer for disbursement to noteholders and other secured creditors. Given that issued liabilities under securitization are subject to tiering of credit risk (tranching), the amount and order in which the cash manager will distribute payments are prescribed in the transaction documents (priority of payments).

From an arranger's perspective, given the high level of interaction that may be required between the cash manager and trustee in the event of incorrect disbursements, it is considered logical practice to have the same trust shop cover both roles. The cash manager has an additional task: to prepare and distribute an investor report to the trustee and other secured parties (including the noteholders).

In some instances, the seller opts to take on the cash manager role and trust shops are asked to act in the role of standby cash manager. This could be either in a "cold" or a "hot" state. A cold standby cash manager would, at closing, commit to being in a position to be the standby cash manager with 30 days' notice. Obviously, for a monthly paying deal this would mean that, should the cash manager default, there would in all likelihood be no one to perform the function on the following payment date. Alternatively, the hot standby cash manager would be fully prepared to step into the role from the outset. The primary tool the cash manager would need to have in place in order to perform the role is a working cash flow model reflecting the transaction structure and payment priorities.

For illustrative purposes, we show the basic breakdown of a cash flow model for a static synthetic CDO. This is done via Excel spreadsheets and is described in Chapter 5.

Account Bank   Amounts collected by the servicer from the underlying assets will first go into a servicer collection account. Depending on the rating of this servicer, these amounts will then be swept to the issuer's account (the issuer transaction account) either on a daily/weekly basis or just prior to an interest payment date. This issuer transaction account is held with the account bank and as such, the account bank will need to meet certain minimum rating criteria.

For transactions featuring a triple-A rated (or even a double-A rated) issuance, the account bank must have short-term ratings of A-1, P-1 or F1 (each agency rating the transaction will point to its minimum level). Short-term ratings rather than long-term ones apply here because the account bank will, at least for the collected amounts, be holding the issuer's cash for only a relatively short period of time (a maximum of one collection period).

The account bank will also be holding cash being used to fund the reserve (cash reserve, commingling reserve, etc.) for the issuer. These amounts can be quite substantial in sum, so the level of the interest rate earned on the issuer's accounts is an important consideration when choosing the account bank.

The documents will provide guidance on how the account bank can invest any cash amounts it holds. These could, in theory, be expanded to generate higher returns, but for rated transactions, the criterion is, as would be expected, restricted to liquid short-term instruments.

Typical investment language for rated ABS is as follows:

- Euro-denominated gilt-edged securities once the issuer or the guarantor of such securities has a short-term senior debt rating of at least Prime-1 (Moody's), A-1+ (S&P) and F1 (Fitch).
- Euro-denominated demand or time deposits, certificates of deposit, and short-term debt obligations (including commercial paper) of any bank or

guaranteed by a bank having a short-term senior debt rating of at least Prime-1 (Moody's), A-1+ (S&P) and F1 (Fitch), provided that in all cases either such investments (1) have a maturity date of 30 business days or less and mature on or before the next following interest payment date, or (2) may be broken or demanded by the issuer (at no cost to the issuer) on or before the next following interest payment date.

Servicer   Throughout the life of the transaction, a servicer will need to be in place to service the portfolio on behalf of the issuer. The servicing role requires not only collecting and recording payments by underlying borrowers, but also the implementation of a process to deal with nonpayment or partial payment under the loans. This extends to managing the process of foreclosure under the loans. Credit rating agencies and investors alike will look for the servicer to demonstrate experience and success in performing these tasks efficiently.

In Europe, typically this function remains with the originator, because it makes most sense that the entity servicing the asset the day before closing is also the servicer the day after closing. This is not a formality, however, and the servicer will be subject to due diligence. If, for example, the rating agencies are concerned by its ability to service the asset portfolio effectively, particularly in a stressed scenario, they may ask that backup arrangements be put in place ahead of closing. Should no backup arrangements be contemplated, the trustee would be charged with finding a replacement servicer should the initial servicer no longer be able to perform the role. The credit rating agencies will also assess how easy it would be for another entity to come in and effectively plug in to the system architecture. A proprietary asset management system will be more difficult (with reliance on documented procedures) to service for the backup provider than industry-wide servicing platforms and systems.

We supply here a checklist of questions that should be put to a servicer when assessing their suitability for a transaction.

Servicer engagement: Diligence questions

- Loan status and collection.
- What are the servicer's general policies and procedures for servicing and collection?
- Historically (last five years) and on average, what percent is lost on each defaulted loan?
- What have been the declines in market value of the {underlying security applicable}?
- As a percentage, what are the historical defaults for the last five years (i.e., loans that are actually foreclosed on)?
- Is servicing centralized in your institution?

- What is the number of delinquent loans per servicing employee?
- What legal costs are involved? Do you use an in-house counsel?
- Do you have the systems capability to transfer servicing to an unaffiliated entity? If so, how long would it take and how much would it cost?
- Do collection procedures vary depending on the stage of delinquency? If so, how?
- How large is the collection staff? What is their average experience level? How are they compensated (salary plus bonus for successful collections, straight salary, or some other means)? What ratio of loans to collectors is maintained for each stage of delinquency?
- What level of supervision is applied to collectors? How are the supervisors compensated?
- How are delinquent loans assigned to collectors? How long do delinquent accounts stay with collectors?
- Depending on the loan's location, what collection options are available to you?
- What options are available to resolve delinquent or defaulted loans?
- What are the procedures to deal with borrowers who file for bankruptcy (or the local equivalent)?
- What is the company's policy and experience regarding loan modification and forbearance?
- Do you have a separate servicing department for loans in arrears?
- How large is your team of arrears staff?
- How are arrears defined? Discuss computer tracking of arrears.
- Explain the collection procedure for arrears. When/how often is a delinquent borrower contacted? How is he or she contacted? Is all collection activity done in house? If not, when are outside collectors used?
- Are arrears and defaults seasonal?
- Describe the primary causes of arrears and defaults. Do they increase with larger loans? Are they particular to this type of product?
- What are the specific internal procedures for foreclosure?
- What data or documentation is necessary to carry out a foreclosure? Where is it stored? Who is eligible to access it?
- What is the average foreclosure period (from the first day of mortgagor default to distribution of property or security sale proceeds)?
- What are the costs of foreclosure (legal, brokerage fees, etc.)?
- Does the mortgage lender always have the legal right to foreclose on a mortgage? If so, must certain conditions exist? Can any party prevent the lender from foreclosing on the property or security?
- Are foreclosure proceedings (i.e., the timing and steps involved) regulated by law?

- Explain the procedures and parties involved (a court, governmental body, etc.) in a foreclosure.
- Is the sale of the property or security carried out through public auction or through a broker? If through auction, explain the auction process.
- Aside from prior lien holders, who else has a right to the security sale proceeds (tax authorities, the courts, etc.)?
- Is the lender entitled to full recovery of the mortgage obligation (outstanding principal, accrued interest, and legal fees) or are its rights to foreclosure proceeds limited to an absolute amount or percent? Conversely, is the lender entitled to any gains realized from the property sale?
- Is a mortgagor personally liable for any unsatisfied mortgage obligation if foreclosure proceeds are insufficient to fully pay off the obligation?
- Does the mortgage lender always have the legal right to foreclose on a mortgage? If so, must certain conditions exist? Can any party (creditors, mortgagors, tenants, etc.) prevent the lender from foreclosing on the property?
- List the information technology requirements for the servicer's operations.
- Describe the main systems infrastructure of the servicer.
- Does the servicer maintain a central computer system supporting financial, client management, distribution, purchasing, and operating activities?
- Is any part of the servicer's business likely to be affected by technological developments? Technical assistance agreements?
- Please give details of new technology purchased in the last three years and proposed to be purchased in the current year and in the future.
- Mention the connectivity of the servicer's network of offices, server's capabilities, and IT installations.
- Discuss the catastrophe recovery capabilities and procedures.
- Is software a purchased package or was it developed in house?
- Do computer backup facilities exist?
- Is a daily backup procedure in place?
- What are the procedures for disaster recovery?
- Can/will the system identify securitized loans?
- Can the system break down the portfolio by loan characteristics?
- Can the system provide historical data on performance with respect to delinquencies, defaults, and prepayments?

Collections Exhibit 3.6 illustrates the collections process undertaken by the servicer.

Reporting Exhibit 3.7 illustrates the reporting process undertaken by the servicer.

In the context of the transaction, the servicer will be responsible for collecting payments on the securitized portfolio, managing nonperforming

EXHIBIT 3.6   Servicer collections process

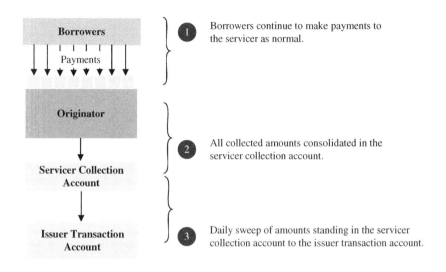

assets, and providing periodic reporting for the trustee, credit rating agencies, and any secured creditors. Though the securitized loans will be flagged on the internal systems of a servicer, those employees charged with collection and arrears management should not be able to identify a securitized loan and a non-securitized loan.

The servicer will prepare a report for each collection period and make this available to the cash manager. A sample reporting template is shown in Exhibit 3.8.

EXHIBIT 3.7   Servicer reporting process

EVENT	Collection Amounts Determined	Replenishment Assets Selected	Servicer Report Distributed	Waterfall Calculation	Interest Amounts Released	Investor Report Distributed
BY	Servicer	Originator	Servicer	Cash Manager	Paying Agent	Cash Manager
FOR	Originator	Cash Manager	Cash Manager/ Raters	Paying Agent	Investors	Investors/ Raters

EXHIBIT 3.8 Servicer reporting template

	CURRENT PERIOD		CUMULATIVE	
	NUMBER OF LOANS	AMOUNT	NUMBER OF LOANS	AMOUNT
-A- AGGREGATE PRINCIPAL OUTSTANDING BALANCE OF PERFORMING AND IN ARREARS LOAN/BOND LOANS				
A.1 AT THE BEGINNING OF CURRENT DETERMINATION PERIOD				
A.2 SCHEDULED AND PAID REPAYMENTS				
A.3 PREPAYMENTS				
A.4 PRINCIPAL RECEIPTS (A2+A3)				
A.5 REPURCHASED LOAN AMOUNTS DUE TO BREACH OF REPS (Principal)				
A.6 REPLACEMENT LOAN AMOUNTS (Principal)				
A.7 MATURED LOAN AMOUNTS (BY INITIAL CURRENT BALANCE)				
A.8 SUBSEQUENT LOANS				
A.9 DEFAULTED LOAN AMOUNTS				
A.T AT THE END OF THE CURRENT DETERM. PERIOD (A1-A4-A5+A6-A9)				
AT THE END OF THE CURRENT DETERM. PERIOD (AT+A10)				

-B- NON-PRINCIPAL RECEIPTS FROM PERFORMING OR IN ARREARS LOAN/BOND LOANS

	CURRENT PERIOD		CUMULATIVE	
	NUMBER OF LOANS	AMOUNT	NUMBER OF LOANS	AMOUNT
B.1 INTEREST FROM INSTALLMENTS AND ARREARS INTEREST				
B.2 INTEREST FROM WHOLE PREPAYMENTS (EARLY CANCEL.)				
B.3 INTEREST FROM REPURCHASED LOANS				
B.4 TOTAL INTEREST RECEIPTS (B1+B2+B3)				
B.5 TOTAL PREPAYMENTS PENALTIES RECEIVED				
B.T TOTAL NON-PRINCIPAL RECEIPTS (B4+B5)				

-C- CASH AMOUNT AVAILABLE FOR PURCHASING SUBSEQUENT LOAN/BOND LOANS

	CURRENT PERIOD		CUMULATIVE	
	NUMBER OF LOANS	AMOUNT	NUMBER OF LOANS	AMOUNT
C.1 CASH FROM PRINCIPAL RECEIPTS (=A4)				
C.3 + EXCESS CASH FROM REPLACEMENT LOANS (A5-A6)				
C.4 − CASH USED FOR SUBSEQUENT LOANS (A8)				
C.T AT THE END OF CURRENT DETERMINATION PERIOD				

The cash manager will then use the information contained in the report as a basis for payment date calculations. Where transactions feature a revolving period, these are often subject to stop replenishment triggers. These triggers will typically include performance triggers such that a certain level of arrears or defaults will constitute an early amortization event under the documents.

Auditor   Information on the portfolio to be securitized is largely drawn from the loan tape provided by the originator to the transaction. The credit rating agencies and investors will base their analysis on this, as will the arranger when calculating weighted average lives and putting together stratification tables for the prospectus. As such, it is good practice to arrange for a verification of the loan tape by an (independent) audit firm. This is not undertaken solely to deal with the risk of fraud (although there have been a number of such cases involving mortgage pools in the United States), but also to identify unintentional mistakes in the loan file attributable to issues with the originator's reporting process.

Although there will be a number of iterations of the loan file, it is sufficient to conduct an audit on the larger pool from which the securitization pool will be drawn. This way, the final pool sold into the vehicle will have formed part of the population that had been subject to audit. To the extent that the originator does not change the process or systems used for data extraction, months elapsing between the dates the checks were performed and the transaction closing date do not typically create any material additional risk.

In terms of process, the arranger will select an audit firm (typically again through an RFP) to complete the work, with the primary considerations being cost, availability of resources to do so in the time available, and the level of the liability cap the auditor will agree to. Liability caps and other terms of engagement are negotiated between the audit firm, the issuer, and the arranger.

The verification of the loan tape information is not an audit *per se*, rather an AUP (agreed-upon procedures) engagement. The distinction is that an audit requires the audit firm to issue an opinion on the work when complete, whereas no such formal opinion is required in this case. For an AUP engagement, the arranger will ask for the auditor to report on its findings from an agreed-upon list of specific procedures (read tests) performed on the loan file.

There is no standard list of tests or questions, so the auditor will rely on the arranger's taking responsibility that the requested procedures are fit for the purpose. As such, access to the report is generally restricted to the arranger and issuer. It is common for the arranger to also check with the credit rating agencies if they would like to see the list of procedures in advance, to see if there are any that need to be added for their comfort.

As a general rule, loan characteristics that relate to static information, for example, original loan balance and original loan term, can be checked against the underlying contract documentation. Dynamic information such as information that has changed since the contract was entered into (e.g., current loan amount or remaining term), can be checked against the data systems, contract schedules, or a combination of both.

In addition to these procedures, the sample size also has to be agreed on. Most securitization portfolios will have a population size numbering in the thousands, so the auditor will take only a randomly selected sample of the loans to make procedural checks on. Consequently, in order to determine the reasonableness of the findings, the arranger will need to communicate the desired confidence interval and acceptable margin of error for the tests. The term confidence interval reflects the degree of comfort that the sample size reflects the population. Margin of error is effectively the level of precision between the sample values and actual population values. For AAA-rated public ABS deals, a 99 percent confidence interval is typically selected, although 95 percent confidence intervals have also been used. In addition a margin of error between one and five percent is used.

The higher the confidence interval, the higher the sample size, but with portfolios reaching the tens of thousands of loans, at some point the increase in statistical accuracy is not worth the additional cost. For a large mortgage pool, a sample size of 400 is often thought of as the most cost-efficient sample size.

SUMMARY AND CONCLUSIONS

The process of closing a securitization transaction is essentially a project management one, with simultaneous action involving a number of third parties as well as the originator. It is important to remember that a securitization SPV has to be set up as a viable company, empowered with the tools to function and effectively perform its obligations vis-à-vis the noteholders. The arranger's involvement is largely over once the vehicle has become live, so the critical process of appointing third-party agents is one that warrants appropriate care and consideration. The arranger has to ensure that those selected to perform roles are not only capable, but can provide experience and know-how at a cost that won't be too onerous on the SPV going forward.

Some roles are more fiduciary in nature and the quantum of financial risk for noteholders is expected to be less. For these, the arranger can rely on more visible metrics when engaging such as reputation, experience, and market visibility.

Other roles, such as that of the servicer, demand a more cautious approach. Servicer performance is central to the noteholders' objective of maximizing asset returns. Consequently, further due diligence is required here. As market and consumer behavior evolves, the successful servicer will have a knack of sensing a shift in landscape and adapting accordingly. Many investors will want to be kept aware of material changes to their transaction servicer's strategy or process. Given that in many instances, the servicer is also the originator, this dialogue is welcome, as retaining investor confidence is vital for the success of potential future market issuance.

CHAPTER 4

The Rating Agency Process and Legal Review

In this chapter we describe the process for the most important stage of the securitization transaction, that of arranging the credit rating agency review and the legal review. These two undertakings, which for the most part occur in parallel (the legal drafting process begins before the ratings review process), are also certainly the most fee-intensive part of the securitization proceedings.

SELECT RATING AGENCIES

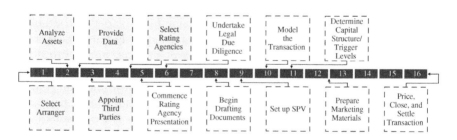

The credit rating agencies are engaged by the issuer to assign ratings to the issued bonds, in order to provide investors with an indication of the relative creditworthiness of the bonds (and so facilitate the sale). Ratings, however, are not intended to be a prediction of default or loss.

Standard & Poor's and Fitch generally assign a rating as to the likelihood of default or first dollar of loss; that is, a shortfall of even $1.00 in repayment of the bond is considered a default. Moody's, however, assigns their ratings based on the concept of expected loss. They state that "Expected loss is a function of the probability of default and the expected severity of loss given default." The rating is determined by comparing the expected loss to an idealized loss table of expected loss by maturity published by Moody's.

In terms of process, the issuer and arranger of the transaction will begin discussion with the rating agencies at the outset of the transaction. The rating agencies will typically have a due diligence meeting with a new issuer to understand their business model, operations, and credit and servicing procedures, as these will have a bearing on the future performance of the portfolio of assets underlying the transaction. For an existing issuer they will want to know how the issuer's business model and operations may have changed since the last issuance.

The credit rating agencies will then undertake an analysis of the asset portfolio, the legal structure, and the liability structure of the transaction. As part of undertaking the portfolio analysis they will require a file with the portfolio data and may also expect to receive historical performance data for the assets, which will be compared to the historical performance of similar assets (as detailed earlier). The product of the portfolio analysis will be base case expected defaults and loss severity for the portfolio. These are specific to each transaction for the portfolio of assets backing the transaction.

The review and analysis of the liability structure includes the creation of a cash flow model that replicates the priority of payments waterfall specifying to whom, and in what priority, the cash flows from the asset portfolio are applied. Portfolio cash flows are projected and applied according to the waterfall to assess the payment of interest and ultimate repayment of principal on the bonds. The base case defaults and loss severity from the portfolio analysis are used as a starting point for a variety of stressed scenarios that include a range of portfolio default rates but also stresses as to the timing of defaults, loss severity, recovery timing, and a range of prepayment and interest rate forecasts.

Hence, the credit rating agencies will examine how the bonds will perform under a range of adverse scenarios and the likelihood of the payment of interest when due and the repayment of principal. For a bond to be assigned a AAA rating, it must be able to withstand greater adverse scenarios than a BBB-rated bond, for example. To the extent that a bond is failing certain scenarios, more credit enhancement in the form of subordinated lower-rated notes or a reserve fund may be necessary. Note that a liquidity facility does not provide credit enhancement, but is simply intended to be available to cover short-term shortfalls in portfolio revenue cash flows to pay interest on the bonds.

The credit rating agencies must also be satisfied that counterparties to the transaction such as swap providers or liquidity facility providers are sufficiently stable and financially strong enough to be able to fulfill their role in the transaction until its maturity.

During their analysis, the credit rating agencies will provide feedback to the issuer of the bonds so that, if necessary, structural changes can be made to improve the bonds' expected ratings. Thus, the process of structuring the transaction is an iterative one of optimizing the structure to balance the needs and requirements of the issuer, the rating agencies, and investors.

The final part of the rating agency review is the presentation by the originator and arranger to the rating agency. This is a formal presentation by representatives of all the relevant departments of the originator describing the assets, organization, and transaction structure.

We provide an example of a typical rating agency presentation pack at Exhibit 6.13 of the book.

UNDERTAKING LEGAL DUE DILIGENCE

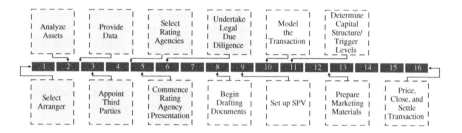

For virtually all securitization transactions, some element of analysis of the contracts that govern the receivables in question is required before the transaction can proceed. In this section we explain the scope and purpose of such a contract due diligence exercise.

As noted earlier in the book, the amount and certainty of future cash flows is at the heart of a receivables securitization. The modeling work required to demonstrate the expected cash flows (based on observed historical data and certain forward-looking assumptions) is of no added value if there is any deficiency in the underlying contracts that results in the receivables not being collectible in their expected amounts and at the expected times. Therefore, it is essential to ensure that this process is carried out as effectively and as robustly as possible. We provide a checklist of key issues for the structurer or arranger.

Who Conducts the Due Diligence?

The contract review exercise is generally conducted by one or more law firms qualified to practice in the jurisdiction whose law governs the contracts in question. These would typically be the law firms involved in the transaction more generally, but this is not necessarily the case. Depending on the combination of firm, jurisdiction, and type of receivable under consideration, it may also be necessary to involve specialist firms to assist with the review.

What Documents Are Reviewed?

The starting point of the review will be the contract or contracts that are used to document the obligation to make payment or repayment of the receivables in question. For a small portfolio of receivables, every contract would be reviewed. For a larger, more granular portfolio, such as an RMBS or credit card ABS, it would not be possible to review the contracts relating to every receivable, so the review is instead done on each of the standard forms used to originate the relevant receivables. In addition, in the transaction documentation there would be a representation from the originator that the receivables in question were originated on the terms of such standard forms.

In addition to the core receivables contracts, it may also be necessary to review other documents. For receivables that are secured, for example, it would be necessary to review the security documentation. For receivables that are consumer assets, it would also be necessary to review the paperwork used in connection with the sales and origination process, such as any marketing materials and any summary terms and conditions. The significance of these is considered further later in the chapter.

It is worth noting at this point the distinction between this contract (legal) due diligence, and the work done (typically by a firm of accountants) as part of the pool audit. That audit work (which is explained further elsewhere in the book) does not examine the substantive terms of the documents in question; rather, it is intended to ensure (based on a representative sample) that the data provided with respect to the receivables corresponds to the information contained in the originator's files.

What Is the Output of the Review?

Once they have completed their review of the documentation and all relevant legislation, the law firm will generally deliver a written report detailing their findings. This would list the documents reviewed, outline the scope of the review, confirm the extent to which the contracts meet the requirements of any applicable legislation and highlight any ways in which the contracts are defective. The report is generally addressed to the originator of the receivables and, sometimes, to the investment banks that are acting as arrangers or lead managers of the transaction. Those banks will review the report addressed to them so that they have recourse to the author of the report in the event that the report contains errors as a result of any negligence. Market practice as to whether or not the liability of the author to the recipients of the report is the subject of a liability cap varies from jurisdiction to jurisdiction, but the trend is toward such caps being included.

It is important that any weaknesses or potential vulnerabilities highlighted by the contract review are properly disclosed in the prospectus or other offering document. Insufficient disclosure of any such concerns (including in the "risk factors" section) may result in the issuer (and any parties who have responsibility for the accuracy of the offering document under the applicable securities law regime) failing to meet their obligation to disclose all information that is material to a potential investor's decision whether or not to invest in the securities issued as part of the transaction. This can result in the relevant parties being liable to compensate investors for any losses incurred in connection with the transaction. In addition to the financial recourse that the addressees of the report might have to the author, the mere fact that the report was sought and obtained can help the arrangers and lead managers to build the "due diligence defense" to securities law actions flowing from inadequate disclosure.

What Areas Does the Review Cover?

The precise scope of the review will vary depending on jurisdiction and on the nature of the receivable, but there are five broad areas to consider.

1. Certainty of Payable Amount The reviewer of the receivable contracts will be asked to confirm that the amounts payable under the contracts are fixed (or calculable by reference to some defined factor, such as an interest rate or index level) and not capable of being reduced in any circumstances. There are several ways in which the payable amount might be the subject of a reduction.

The first is a failure by the other party to the contract (that is, in general, the originator) to meet its obligations. The concern is that such a failure might result in the obligor no longer being obliged to make payments on the receivable. This is a risk on any contract where the originator's obligations are not fully performed at the time of the securitization, which is why the majority of securitizations involve contracts that are fully performed from the originator's perspective, such as a fully drawn loan (where the only meaningful ongoing obligations are the payment of interest and the repayment of principal by the borrower). A review of the contract would establish whether there are any ongoing obligations on the part of the originator, and enable a determination of the likelihood of the originator failing to fulfill any such obligation, with the consequences described previously.

The second way in which the payable amount might be reduced is by setoff. An obligor's right to set off might arise within the receivables contract, or between the receivables contract and some other financial transaction. In the former case, the concern is that the obligor would seek to set off its obligation to make payment against the contractual counterparty's obligation to make payment under the same contract. This might arise, for example, where a loan agreement contains an obligation to make further advances; the risk is that if the originator fails to fund such a further advance, the obligor could set off his obligation to make a repayment against the originator's obligation to make that further advance. In the latter case, the concern is that the obligor would seek to set off its obligation to make payment against the contractual counterparty's obligation to make some other payment to it. This might arise, for example, where the borrower of a mortgage loan also has a bank account with the lender; the risk is that the borrower would seek to set off his obligation to make a payment on the mortgage loan against the lender's obligation to return the fund's standing to the credit of the bank account. The aim of the review in this area would be to determine whether or not the contract in question contains language prohibiting the obligor from asserting any right of setoff.

The third way in which the payable amount might be reduced is the operation of any conditions to payment. For a receivable to be capable of being the subject of a securitization, it will be necessary that the payment obligation not be a conditional one, and the contract due diligence is the means of confirming that this is the case.

Finally, the reviewer will be asked whether there are any deficiencies or ambiguities in the operative provisions that could result in the payable amount not being what the originator expected it to be.

2. Asset Transferability   The second area that the reviewer will be asked to consider is the transferability or assignability of the asset in question. The aim is to establish that the sale of the receivable to the issuing special purpose vehicle (SPV) as part of the transaction can occur without notifying and/or seeking the consent of any party to the contract constituting the receivable. A loan agreement may contain, for example, restrictions on the nature or location of transferees in order to preserve a position in which no withholding tax is payable on interest payments on the loan.

In the event that an actual sale of the receivables is not possible, it may still be possible to effect a synthetic securitization of those receivables, but even that could potentially be restricted by the terms of the contract.

The due diligence would provide advice on what restrictions, if any, apply, and a list of what consents must be sought and what notifications must be made.

3. Disclosure of Information   The third area that would sometimes be covered by the contract due diligence is the question of whether or not the issuer (when it becomes the owner of the receivable) has the right to disclose information on the performance of the receivable to third parties. The issuer needs this freedom so that it is able to publish periodic reports for noteholders (or, more precisely, so that the servicer can prepare and publish such reports on the issuer's behalf). In the event that the contracts do contain confidentiality provisions that would prohibit the publication of specific information, it may still be possible for the issuer to publish aggregated (and therefore anonymized) data on the performance of the portfolio as a whole.

4. Enforceability   The fourth (and perhaps most important) part of the contract due diligence is an assessment of the enforceability of the contract in question. The starting point will be a simple analysis of whether the contract appears capable of being enforced under the applicable governing law, which is normally a relatively straightforward matter so long as the terms of the contract are sufficiently certain and the subject matter is not something likely to run afoul of public policy in the relevant jurisdiction.

For certain classes of asset, the analysis is much more complicated. This is particularly true of consumer assets (mortgage loans, unsecured loans, credit card receivables, and so on), as they are generally the subject of legislation intended to protect the consumer. The operation of the legislation varies from country to country and the detail is outside the scope of this book, but it is often the case that a failure to comply with the legislation will result in the contract being unenforceable (in whole or in part), or enforceable only with a court order, the cost of obtaining which might well outweigh the value recovered. Consumer protection legislation can prescribe a particular form that a consumer credit agreement must take, can prohibit the inclusion of terms that are unfair to the consumer, and can require that numerical information be calculated and presented in a certain way. Often the legislation is somewhat draconian and even immaterial failures to comply can result in unenforceability. The information made available to the consumer at the time of origination (such as any marketing material or documents containing summary terms and conditions) can also have an impact on enforceability, and the reviewing law firm will have to assume that nothing was said during the sales process that was inconsistent with the terms of the contract or prohibited by the relevant rules. In addition, some jurisdictions have laws that seek to prevent usury by setting a limit on the rates of interest that can be charged on particular asset classes.

The consideration of enforceability is the area of the due diligence that is likely to be the most time consuming and that may require the involvement of a specialist law firm familiar with all relevant legislation. In some cases the analysis is fairly mechanical (for example, was numerical information presented in the specified way?) but in other cases a degree of judgment is required (for example, is a particular term unfair to the consumer?). It is rare for a consumer asset to get an entirely clean bill of health, and a degree of pragmatism is sometimes required, as experience shows that technical deficiencies are not widely understood or relied on by consumers in practice. It is imperative, however, that any deficiencies are properly described in the offering document in order to avoid liability for inadequate disclosure.

5. Taxes The law firm conducting the contract due diligence may also be asked to advise on whether or not any taxes or duties would be payable in connection with the transfer of the receivables and any associated re-registration of accompanying security interests. That analysis is, strictly speaking, not part of the contract due diligence, but is often done at around the same time and by the same advisors.

BEGIN DRAFTING DOCUMENTS

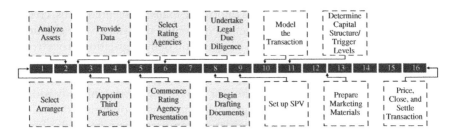

The next stage is the drafting of the formal legal documents that describe the transaction and also the rights and obligations of the various parties that will be involved at the closing. We describe the different types of official documents that are needed, and also their content.

Legal Opinions

This section describes the process of obtaining legal opinions as part of a securitization transaction and gives an overview of what such a legal opinion might cover. The legal work performed as part of the contract due diligence is described in the contract due diligence section.

The law firm(s) involved in a securitization will be asked to confirm in writing the advice that they have given as part of the transaction. This advice is given in formal documents known as legal opinions. The giving of a legal opinion results in the law firm(s) having liability to the addressees of that opinion in the event that it negligently misstates the legal position. Law firms are mindful of the importance of this process and generally organize internal committees that review the contents of all legal opinions prior to their being given, in order to ensure consistency between transactions and to protect the firm from negligence actions. Legal opinions are expressed to be correct as at the date they are given, and are not intended to provide any assurance about the future state of the law. In the event more than one jurisdiction is relevant (such as, for example, where a transaction party is incorporated in one jurisdiction and enters into documents governed by the law of a different jurisdiction), it is likely that legal opinions will be required from law firms in each jurisdiction.

Legal opinions generally have four main sections: background, assumptions, opinions, and reservations (although the order of these sections and the precise terminology used can vary).

The background section typically contains an outline description of the transaction and identifies the party who has asked the law firm to provide the opinion. It will also list the transaction documents in respect of which the opinion is given.

The assumptions section contains a list of factual matters that the law firm has relied on as being true in arriving at its opinion. This list might include facts about the transaction parties (such as their tax residency, their intention in entering into the transaction and their solvency), facts about the transaction documents (such as the genuineness of signatures and the conformity of originals to the copies reviewed) and facts about the law of jurisdictions other than the one in respect of which the opinion is given (such as the enforceability of the documents under that governing law and the operation of the insolvency regime in that jurisdiction). One important aspect in reviewing legal opinions is to ensure that the assumptions made by the law firm correspond to the actual position, and in particular, that assumptions made about the law of other jurisdictions are supported by legal advice obtained from firms qualified to practice in those jurisdictions.

The opinions section contains the law firm's view on the points of law on which it has been asked to opine. Some examples of the matters commonly covered by legal opinions include the following:

- The transaction parties have the capacity and authority to enter into the transaction documents and those documents have been duly executed.
- The obligations assumed by the transaction parties are legal, valid, binding, and enforceable.
- The transaction parties are duly incorporated (as companies) and validly existing under relevant law (and, where the relevant jurisdiction has such a concept, those parties are in good standing).

- The choice of governing law will be respected.
- No consents or regulatory approvals are required in connection with the transaction (other than those that have already been obtained).
- The transaction security is valid and effective.
- No stamp duty or similar tax is payable in connection with the execution, delivery, or performance of the transaction documents.

The reservations section lists exceptions from the law firm's opinions (often referred to as "carve-outs") and a description of relevant areas in which the law firm believes the law is uncertain. These reservations must be reviewed carefully, as they can fundamentally alter the effect of a firm's opinion.

In addition to these general matters, securitization legal opinions also cover some deal-specific points that are material to the effectiveness of the transaction. The most important of these additional opinions is that the transfer of the assets to the SPV constitutes a true sale. This means that the transaction would be analyzed by a court as a sale of the assets and would not be recharacterised as a loan secured on those assets. This provides comfort that in the event the seller of the assets (that is, in general, the originator) subsequently becomes insolvent, the assets will not be considered to be part of the bankruptcy estate and will remain available to the SPV and its creditors.

Transaction Documentation

Here we describe the documents commonly used to establish and administer a securitization transaction. The detail of these documents is outside the scope of this book, but the following is an overview of the documents and how they operate. The documents are drafted by the law firm(s) involved in the transaction, and are commented on by the other parties, including the seller/originator, the rating agencies, the trustee, and (to the extent relevant) the hedging counterparty.

> **Asset Sale Agreement** The starting point is generally a form of sale and purchase agreement pursuant to which the receivables are sold by the originator to the SPV. The precise form of the agreement will depend on the asset class and jurisdiction in question. One important feature of this document will be the representations and warranties given with respect to the receivables by the seller, as it is these representations and warranties that give the SPV recourse to the seller in the event the receivables are not as described (either through a buyback mechanism or through damages for misrepresentation).

Servicing Agreement There will be a servicing or administration agreement pursuant to which the servicer is appointed by the SPV to administer the portfolio of receivables on the SPV's behalf. This document would commonly contain a list of the services that the servicer will provide in relation to the receivables, and will establish the standard to which those services must be performed.

Note Trust Deed As with any capital markets transaction, there will also be a trust deed that constitutes, and establishes the terms and conditions of, the notes to be issued by the SPV. This will contain all of the positive and negative covenants given by the SPV that help with the bankruptcy remoteness analysis described in the section on SPVs.

Issuer Security Document There would be one or more documents creating security over all of the SPV's assets (including the receivables) to secure the SPV's obligations to the noteholders and the SPV's other creditors. This agreement, which is sometimes called an issuer security document or a deed of charge, will, among other things, prescribe the order in which proceeds from enforcing the security are applied to meet the SPV's various secured obligations.

Subscription Agreement There would be a subscription or underwriting agreement pursuant to which the SPV commits to issuing the notes and the lead managers agree to subscribe to the notes so that they can sell them on to the market as part of the transaction. This is perhaps the most important document for the investment bank(s) carrying on the lead manager role as it contains various protections, including representations from the SPV and the originator as to the sufficiency of disclosure, and indemnification for any loss suffered by those banks. It would also contain the provisions dealing with the banks' fees.

Agency Agreements There will be a series of documents appointing each of the agents of the SPV, such as the paying agent and account bank.

Swap Agreements Any hedging transactions entered into by the SPV would, in general, be documented using the standard documentation published by the International Swaps and Derivatives Association Inc., but with amendments to reflect the fact that the hedging is being entered into as part of a structured finance transaction. For transactions involving rated notes, these hedging contracts will include certain provisions demanded by the rating agencies to the effect that in the event the credit rating of the hedging counterparty falls below a defined level, it is required to take certain action, such as the posting of collateral or the obtaining of a guarantee.

Prospectus

Although not a transaction document (in that it has no contractual force), making an offer of securities to the public generally requires the publication of a prospectus or equivalent offering document. This document contains all information regarding the transaction and the receivables that a potential investor would require in order to make its investment decision.

SET UP THE SPV

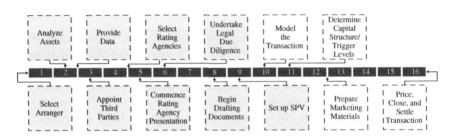

The next step, or one that occurs simultaneously while the legal opinions are being drafted, is the incorporation of the SPV. We describe the various steps that must be undertaken as part of this process.

SPV Incorporation

At the center of virtually every cash securitization transaction is the issuance of debt securities by a company established for the purposes of the transaction. These companies are commonly referred to as special purpose vehicles or special purpose entities; we will refer to them as SPVs.

Although the SPV is something of a passive entity, in that it is merely the conduit through which the transaction cash flows pass, the way in which it is established and administered is an important element in the structuring of a securitization transaction. In this section we outline the key considerations that need to be taken into account with respect to the SPV, and explain their significance.

Jurisdiction

The first question to be answered is, in which jurisdiction should the SPV be incorporated? This choice can be influenced by several factors. Possibly the most important factor is taxation, which is relevant in two main respects.

First, it will be necessary to consider the taxation of the vehicle itself, and in particular whether it will be liable to pay corporation tax (or the equivalent in the relevant jurisdiction) on its profits. As explained earlier in the book, all of the income received by the SPV will be paid out to noteholders and its other creditors (except, often, for a very small amount, typically immaterial, of profit which is retained in order to provide corporate benefit and to give the SPV substance), so on the face of it there should be little net income on which to levy a tax charge. The position can, however, be complicated by there being timing mismatches between the receipt by the SPV of income and payment by the SPV of its liabilities, which can result in the SPV making a profit in some financial periods and a loss in others. This can also arise as a result of the need to revalue derivative positions by reference to their market value. Some jurisdictions have tax rules that provide a favorable tax regime to securitization SPVs, and the availability of such a regime will be an important consideration in choosing a jurisdiction.

The second consideration is withholding tax. It will be important for the SPV to be able to pay interest and repay principal to noteholders without being required to make a withholding from such payments in order to pay tax to the relevant local authority. Some analysis will be required to see in what jurisdictions the SPV needs to be resident in order for it to be able to pay free of withholding tax to investors located in the jurisdictions in which the notes are offered. There is always a risk that a change of law will result in a withholding requirement being imposed where previously there was none, and this risk might be dealt with by including in the terms and conditions of the notes a call option and/or a put option enabling the issuer or the investors to bring the transaction to an end early in the event such a change in law occurs.

The third factor to consider is the question of in what jurisdictions the SPV can be incorporated (and tax resident) in order for it to be able to hold the assets involved in the transaction. There may be contractual or regulatory restrictions on the transfer of the assets that could mean that transferees have to be located in particular jurisdictions. In addition, it may be necessary that the SPV be tax resident in a particular jurisdiction in order for it to be able to receive payments on the receivables free of any withholding or deduction for tax (which is a slightly different consideration from the point about the SPV being able to make payments free of withholding that was just discussed).

The final consideration is whether the jurisdiction of incorporation is acceptable to the stock exchange on which it is proposed the notes will be listed, and to any relevant listing authority. It is common (although in some cases not required) for the SPV to be incorporated in the jurisdiction in which the notes will be listed.

Constitution and Corporate Formalities

The SPV is normally a private limited company. In some jurisdictions the SPVs are simply companies incorporated under general law. Other jurisdictions have specific legal regimes under which the SPVs are established, and SPVs in those jurisdictions are frequently referred to using the name of the legislation in question (for example, "Law 130" vehicles in Italy and "Section 110" companies in Ireland).

As with all companies, there is generally a requirement that SPVs have one or more directors (or equivalent officers) who are responsible for the management of the company. In practice, these directors are not required to make any decisions other than the decision to enter into the securitization transaction itself. Once the documents relating to that securitization have been entered into, the SPV is more or less on autopilot, with cash flowing in and out and services being provided in accordance with the agreed-on mechanics.

The existence and independence of the SPV company directors are important, however, as they form part of the analysis leading to the conclusion that the SPV is bankruptcy remote. What this means is that the SPV should never become insolvent or enter into any sort of insolvency proceeding and that the insolvency of some other entity (such as the originator) will not affect the solvency of the SPV. The directors are relevant as one way a company can enter into insolvency proceedings is for the directors to pass a resolution to that effect. The SPV will commit, in the documentation it enters into as part of the transaction, to not pass any such resolution, and the directors could therefore only do so by allowing the SPV to commit a breach of contract. The other elements of the bankruptcy remoteness analysis are the use of "orphan" structures and the inclusion of "limited recourse" provisions in the contracts documenting the SPV's liabilities. These two points are considered next.

Orphan companies are so called because they do not have parent companies (or at least not in the conventional sense). This can be achieved by having the shares in the SPV held by a professional trust company on trust, generally for charitable purposes. In some cases, a two-tier structure is used, with the SPV having a holding company whose shares are held on a charitable trust. It is important than an SPV is an orphan company so that it cannot be dragged into the insolvency of some wider group (the SPV will of course also have no subsidiary companies). In addition, its orphan nature means that the SPV's assets and liabilities do not appear on the balance sheet of any other entity, and that it is outside the scope of any restrictions in, for example, the existing financing documents of the originator (such as any restriction on granting security).

Perhaps the most important way in which the solvency of an SPV is preserved is by making all of its liabilities (or at least all of its expected liabilities) limited recourse obligations. This means that the SPV's liabilities are limited in recourse to the cash of the SPV available to meet that liability (that is, all of the SPV's cash on a particular date apart from the cash required to meet higher-ranking obligations then falling due). Payment of all obligations is deferred to the extent cash is not available at the time. This, taken together with the fact the SPV should have no liabilities other than those that are expressed to be limited recourse, should mean that the SPV will never fail to pay its debts as they fall due and will therefore remain solvent.

Licensing

It is always necessary to take legal advice as to whether the entry into the transaction requires the SPV to hold some sort of license or regulatory permission. For example, the holding of consumer credit assets might require a consumer credit license, and the processing of personal information might require an authorization under the applicable data protection legislation.

MODELING THE TRANSACTION

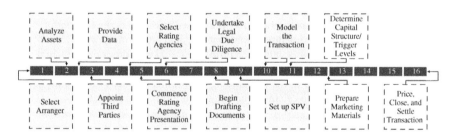

Though credit rating agencies have no active role in structuring a transaction, they are still a key participant and they need to be comfortable with the capital structure and transaction features being put forward for rating. The credit rating agencies will not offer any proposal on what form an optimal capital structure would take. It is up to the arranger to put together a model in order to evaluate for itself the appropriate level of credit enhancement required for each class of notes.

We describe a model that is a hypothetical example of the basic features commonly found in the structure for a European residential mortgage-backed security (RMBS) transaction.

Structure Worksheet

Collateral

Principal Balance — The outstanding principal balance of the loans securing the notes. The notes are sized based on this balance.

Interest Rate — The assumed interest rate of the loans over their life.

Remaining Term — The number of months over which the loans will amortize to zero. It is assumed that all of the loans are fully amortizing with bullet or interest-only redemption types.

Capital Structure

Rated Notes — The notes are sized as percentages of the collateral principal balance.

The notes are floating rate notes and the coupon resets on a quarterly basis equal to 3m Euribor plus the margin.

If the notes are not called on their optional redemption date, the margin over 3m Euribor will step up to the step margin.

Reserve Fund — The reserve fund is sized as a percentage of the total notes. The initial deposit into the reserve fund is based on the initial % whereas the target balance of the reserve fund to be funded from available interest is calculated using the target %.

Fees — The annual fee percentages for the trustee and servicing costs.

Scenario Inputs

Euribor 3 month — The issued notes are assumed to be quarterly pay, floating rate notes. The coupon on the notes equals 3m Euribor + margin.

Prepayments — The annual prepayment rate used to calculate the amount of unscheduled principal that is repaid before maturity as a result of borrowers selling the property or making additional principal payments. This rate is decompounded to a monthly rate that is applied to the outstanding performing balance of the [mortgage] loans to calculate the amount monthly prepayments.

Defaults — The annual default percentage used to calculate the principal amount of loans that will default each year. It is assumed that the underlying collateral will be repossessed and sold.

In this model there are inputs for the default type and also start and end months so that, if desired, defaults will only occur during a set period of time. If the default type is specified as "annual" then new defaults are calculated using the current outstanding performing principal balance. If the default type is "cumulative" defaults are calculated using the original balance of the loans.

Months to Recovery — The number of months between the initial default and the time the property is sold and any recovery amounts are received.

Loss %	The percentage of the defaulted principal that is assumed to be lost when the property is sold. This should include accrued but unpaid interest on the loan, the costs and expenses associated with repossession and sale, as well as any assumed decline in the market value of the collateral.
Optional Redemption	Some transactions have optional redemption provisions that permit the issuer to redeem the notes at its discretion on or after a particular date. These include:
Exercise?	TRUE or FALSE to indicate whether or not an optional redemption provision will be exercised.
Date	The payment date on or after which an optional redemption can be exercised.
Apply step-up?	TRUE or FALSE to indicate whether or not to apply the coupon step-up if the optional redemption is not exercised.
Period (Month) Date	For information only. Has no effect on the calculations.
Factor	The percentage of loans that would be outstanding if there were no defaults or unscheduled principal payments and only scheduled principal payments were made.

Collateral Worksheet

SMM	Single monthly mortality. The decompounded annual prepayment rate $= 1 - (1 - \text{Annual prepayment rate})^{(1/12)}$.
MDR	Monthly default rate. If the default type is set to "annual" then this is the default rate from the structure sheet decompounded to a monthly rate. If the default type is set to "cumulative" then this is the default rate from the structure sheet divided by the number of months over which defaults have been set to occur.
Total Balance	Total outstanding principal balance of the loans (performing and nonperforming).
Performing Balance	The outstanding principal balance of nondefaulted (performing) loans.
[New] Defaults	The principal amount of new defaulted loans in the month.
Foreclosure Balance	The outstanding balance of defaulted, nonperforming loans for which losses and recoveries have not yet occurred.
Interest	The monthly interest received from the performing loans.
(A)DBIRM	The amortized default balance in recovery month. This is the principal balance of loans on repossessed properties that are being sold in the month. It is equal to the amount of new defaults N months ago where N equals the input for months to recovery.

(*continued*)

Losses	The amount of principal losses in the period equal to the DBIRM × Loss severity input. Losses cannot exceed the defaulted principal balance.
Recoveries	Recovered principal from defaulted assets
Actual Sched Prin	Scheduled principal payments received from the performing loans.
Prepayments	Voluntary prepayments of principal (as opposed to recoveries, which are considered non-voluntary prepayments of principal); that is, principal received earlier than its scheduled date.
Total Prin	The sum of Actual scheduled principal received + Voluntary prepayments + Recoveries
Scenario Results	
Initial Excess Spread	The initial excess interest margin of the interest rate on the collateral over the senior expenses and interest to be paid to the bonds.
Principal Loss	The amount of principal losses suffered by each of the rated notes.
Interest Shortfalls	The total amount of unpaid interest on each of the notes. In this model, unpaid interest is not carried forward from quarter to quarter.
WAL	The weighted average life or the weighted average time to be repaid principal expressed in years.
Cumulative Collateral Defaults	The total amount of defaulted loans on the collateral in amount and percentage of the original balance of the collateral.
Cumulative Collateral Losses	The total amount of losses on the collateral after recoveries of principal on defaulted loans have been received.
Sources & Uses	
	Sources & Uses shows how the principal and interest cash flows from the collateral have been applied.

Waterfall Worksheet

The waterfall worksheet aggregates the collateral cash flows on a quarterly basis and applies them to notes according to the priority of payments—the waterfall—specified in the offering circular. This is an example of a sequential waterfall in that items are paid sequentially rather than pro rata. After paying more senior expenses such as trustee and servicing expenses, interest received from the loans is applied sequentially to pay interest first to the class A notes, then to the class B notes, and finally to the class C notes. Similarly, principal received from the loans is applied sequentially to redeem the class A notes, then the class B notes, and finally the class C notes.

This structure also uses the concept of a principal deficiency ledger, which is a mechanism to track the allocation of losses from the underlying collateral to the notes. At the time the notes are issued they are fully secured by the loans supporting the transaction. So, assuming no losses, over time the principal received from the amortizing loans will redeem the notes. However, when there is a loss of principal on the loans this must be addressed in some way; otherwise, the notes will suffer a principal shortfall and, if not eventually cured, a loss at maturity. In this structure, the losses allocated to the notes are tracked in a principal deficiency ledger (PDL). Losses are allocated in reverse sequential order; that is, first to the lowest rated notes, class C; then to the next lowest rated notes, class B; and finally to the most senior rated notes, class A.

Losses are allocated to the class C PDL via a debit to the class C PDL until the debit balance of the class C PDL equals the outstanding principal balance of the class C notes. Following this, further losses are debited to the class B PDL until its debit balance is equal to the class B outstanding balance. Finally, losses will be debited to the class A PDL. A debit balance on the PDL of a class of notes indicates that that class of notes will suffer a principal loss unless the loss that has been allocated is eventually rectified.

In a sequential pay waterfall, included in the waterfall are payments to credit the PDL balances of the notes. Hence, although the interest due on the notes is paid sequentially, losses that have been allocated to more senior notes via the PDL will be covered before interest is paid on more junior notes. As a result, the available revenue funds are paid in the following priority:

1. Senior expenses such as trustee fees and servicing fees.
2. Interest due on the class A notes.
3. Credit the class A PDL an amount up to the debit balance of the class A PDL. The amount so credited is added to available principal funds and the debit balance of the PDL is accordingly reduced.
4. Interest due on the class B notes.
5. Credit the class B PDL an amount up to the debit balance of the class B PDL and add the amount to available principal funds.
6. Interest due on the class C notes.
7. Credit the class C PDL an amount up to the debit balance of the class C PDL and add the amount to available principal funds.
8. To the reserve fund until its balance equals its target amount.
9. Any amount remaining, the excess, to the originator.

Available revenue funds are equal to the sum of interest received from the loans and the amount of money held in the reserve fund. The required balance of the reserve fund is determined by the rating agencies when the transaction is structured to cover potential interest shortfalls and principal losses. During their analysis they may model stressed scenarios under which the interest received from the loans is insufficient by itself to pay the interest on the notes and also cover principal shortfalls. A reserve fund is created as a contingency to cover these types of stressed scenarios.

Available principal funds that are used to redeem the notes equal the sum of principal redemptions received on the loans (scheduled and voluntary prepayments), recoveries of principal from repossessed properties that have been sold, and amounts credited to the principal deficiency ledger. Available principal funds are used to redeem the notes in this sequential order:

1. To redeem the class A notes until their balance is zero.
2. To redeem the class B notes until their balance is zero.
3. To redeem the class C notes until their balance is zero.

DETERMINE CAPITAL STRUCTURE/TRIGGER LEVELS

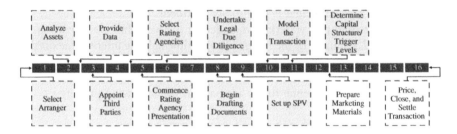

This part of the process is perhaps the most quantitative, and one that is most closely associated with the structuring of the transaction. The capital structure of an ABS transaction describes the form of the SPV liabilities; that is, the ABS notes that are issued. Subjects such as the size of each note tranche, and indeed how many tranches are to be used, are finalized at this stage (although investor demand will influence, and can result in modification of, the final outcome). In this section we describe the process undertaken when arranging the note structure.

Capital Structure

The liabilities structure in a securitization is tiered into one or more tranches offering different combinations of risk and return to the holders of the notes. Most structures are based on sequential pay tranches; that is, the senior notes being repaid with principal collections and notes subordinated to these in each case only being repaid after full repayment of more senior notes. In some instances structures have features with sequential payments switching to pro rata payments (perhaps between the two most senior notes) at some point in time if the transaction performs as expected. Conversely, structures may move to "full turbo" if performance is poor. This is when all collections (principal and interest) are used to repay principal after senior expenses have been met.

When working toward setting the attachment points for the different liability tranches, the following are examples of factors to be considered:

- **Investor appetite for certain levels of risk or maturity.** Investors such as money market funds could be restricted to very short-dated paper or may have internal credit requirements that prohibit them buying paper that is below a certain rating threshold, or buying into a capital structure where the most senior note is not rated AAA. This becomes particularly relevant if the deal is being privately placed and key interested investors have communicated certain minimum requirements that would need to be satisfied ahead of an investment. Alternatively, there may be appetite for risk at lower levels in the capital structure from investors with minimum internal rate of return (IRR) targets, and to the extent economics work, the capital structure would need to be put together to ensure the appropriately risked credit would be offered as part of the transaction.
- **Credit rating agency analysis.** The credit rating agencies providing the credit rating on the liabilities will wish to be confident that the notes will receive timely payment of principal and interest under given stress scenarios. There is always the potential that, for a given portfolio, higher ratings are unachievable. This may be due inter alia to a lack of historical data from a jurisdiction, weaknesses in the structure, or a ceiling given the rating of the sovereign. It is worth also noting that there may be transactions that require more than one rating to attract investors (investors will usually like to see at least one of S&P and Moody's in most cases). Where more than one agency is rating the transaction, it is the more conservative analysis of the agencies that drives the capital structure.
- **Originator motivations.** Post-2008, during the time when the only market in Europe for new issue securitizations was as collateral for repo funding with the European Central Bank (ECB), capital structures featured a senior single-A rated and an unrated subordinated tranche retained by the issuer. As the market returns to greater stability and investor appetite, capital structures will in each instance reflect investor risk-reward profiles at the time. Originators may also be reluctant to fund at high spreads, and so may look to restrict offered bonds at senior and possibly mezzanine levels while retaining junior bonds that would be

EXHIBIT 4.1   Hypothetical capital structure

Class	Rating Equivalent	% of Transaction	Class Balance	WAL	Base Rate	Indicative Spread
A	AAA	90.00%	1,350,000,000	4.50	3 m Euribor	2.00%
B	A	4.00%	60,000,000	6.00	3 m Euribor	3.00%
C	BBB	6.00%	90,000,000	6.00	3 m Euribor	4.00%
		100.00%	1,500,000,000	4.70		2.16%

funded through alternative channels (such as deposits). In some instances, the junior bonds may also be rated to leave open the option of distribution at a later stage.

It is important to note how an originator would see overall running cost for a securitization. We illustrate this in Exhibits 4.1 and 4.2 with a hypothetical capital structure and transaction costs, arriving at an overall weighted average cost over time, which the originator can compare to alternative funding sources.

This preliminary analysis will assist the originators to determine if the economics of the deal are viable.

EXHIBIT 4.2   Hypothetical transaction costs

Upfront Transaction Costs

	EUR
International legal fees (including trustees)	325,000
Local legal fees*	45,000
Rating agency (one)	250,000
Listing fee	3,400
Trustee, PPA, cash manager, listing agent	50,000
SPV management	15,000
Printing	8,000
Collateral and cash flow audit	70,000
Other miscellaneous expenses	10,000
Total upfront fees (excl. VAT)	776,440
Total upfront fees (incl. VAT)	663,567
Expenses as a % of total volume	0.044%
Per annum equivalent cost over average life	0.010%

Ongoing Miscellaneous Costs

	EUR
Trustee, PPA, Cash Manager	10,000
Credit Rating Agency (1)	10,000
Credit Rating Agency (2)	10,000
Credit Rating Agency (3)	10,000
SPV management	10,000
Stock exchange costs*	1,500
Total upfront fees (excl. VAT)	51,500
Total upfront fees (incl. VAT)	58,750

*No VAT chargeable.

All-In Cost (stated as per annum equivalent)

	Cost (% per annum) EUR
Weighted average cost of funds	2.160%
Amortized fees and expenses	0.010%
Interest rate swap intermediation fee (if required)	0.010%
Other ongoing fees (SPV, rating, trustee, etc.)	0.001%
All-in cost per annum (over 3m Euribor)	2.180%

Early Amortization Trigger Levels

A transaction may feature a revolving period if the underlying assets are particularly short dated or there is a desire to extend the term of funding for the overall transaction. A number of transactions will feature a revolving period where, rather than asset redemptions being used to pay off senior liabilities, the principal proceeds are used to purchase further eligible assets from the originator—thus replenishing the pool. For the originator, this has the obvious benefit of extending the duration of the term of the funding and particularly for short-dated assets — some receivables may be as short as 15 days in duration—this is absolutely necessary for a viable transaction.

A revolving period feature will be subject to scrutiny from the rating agencies (and investors) as it introduces additional risk that needs to be mitigated. The key risk is a deterioration of quality in the portfolio, where the assets being sourced in on each replenishment date are of a lower quality, thus diluting the creditworthiness of the entire portfolio. There are a number of conditions that could be introduced to address this: Assets being purchased would certainly be required to meet at least the eligibility of the initial assets sold to the SPV but may also be subject to additional, more rigorous standards. There may be limitations on the type of asset being sourced in to ensure the portfolio composition remains relatively stable, or at the very least, the absolute levels of weaker assets are limited.

The transaction would typically feature early amortization triggers that would cause the revolving period to end, with future redemptions being directed to repayment of liabilities. These early amortization triggers could include, inter alia, the occurrence of a servicer termination event, a reduction in the overall loan-to-value (LTV) ratio or weighted average coupon (WAC) levels for the portfolio, or if the cash reserves carry a shortfall.

Early amortization events typically also include performance triggers, as investors would want to avoid further assets being added to the portfolio where there was a notable decline in the quality of either the new assets or the portfolio as a whole. Additionally, this creates a servicing incentive for the originator. When structuring the transaction and evaluating where these trigger levels should be set, one approach is to take historic performance as a reference. This is particularly useful if these data cover a complete financial cycle.

This approach is illustrated graphically next.

In Exhibit 4.3 we show historical data for a hypothetical originator. We can see largely consistent performance across the portfolio, although vintages 2008 Q3 and 2008 Q4 (dashed lines) are of a poorer quality. Default levels for the first two quarters in 2009 are also elevated. From this it can also be inferred that the signs of poorer performance become apparent around five to six months after origination (circled).

Consequently, we are able then to make the distinction here between typical loss levels and evidence of a worsening quality and create a perform-ance threshold between clusters. This would represent (non) performance trigger levels; that is, cumulative defaults of no more than 2 percent for the first 18 months and no more than 4 percent for months 18–24. This is illustrated at Exhibit 4.4.

If on a particular transaction date in the revolving period, the originator is unable to source sufficient eligible assets, it would be punitive for the revolving period to end immediately (performance of the assets may still be positive). The structure could accommodate for this by holding on to the amounts that would otherwise have been used to purchase assets until the following payment date that sufficient assets could be sourced. This approach does, however, generate negative carry (as cash being held in an account generates lower yield than cash from assets). As such, it makes sense to put a

EXHIBIT 4.3 Portfolio historical profile

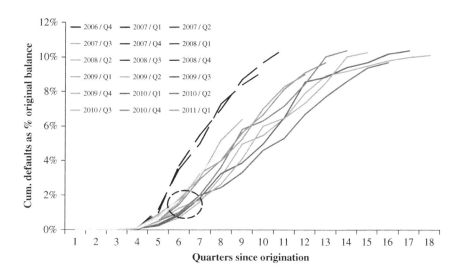

EXHIBIT 4.4 Cumulative defaults profile

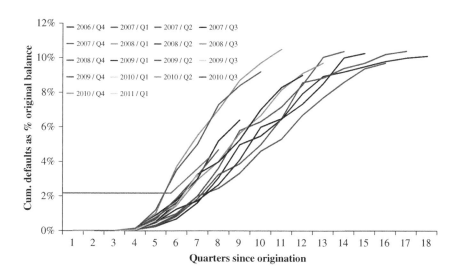

limit on the amount of cash that could be held for this purpose. The limit could take many forms—for example:

- A single cash cap where unused principal proceeds could be set aside up to a capped amount. Should the amount be in excess of this cap, it would trigger an amortization event.
- A staggered cash cap where the cap allows the originator a single breach (to a higher threshold) but where the standard cap applies for the following period.

Alternatively, the liability repayment profile could be controlled with only a portion of the redemption amounts being used to purchase further assets as the bonds are allowed to amortize up to a scheduled amount, rather like a corporate bond with a sinking fund. While its primary purpose is to give investors a predictable payment schedule, it also serves as an alternative to consider where it is envisaged that sourcing sufficient eligible assets may be difficult.

PREPARE MARKETING MATERIALS

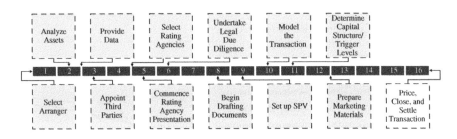

As we move toward a substantially final structure, the arranger, together with other lead managers, begins the process of preparing the transaction for its marketing phase. This phase—often referred to as a road-show—will feature a number of one-to-one meetings with potential advisors and the originator, accompanied by the arranger. The road show is almost always a very busy schedule with back-to-back meetings spanning several days and in several jurisdictions. It gives the originator every opportunity to pitch the transaction and their ability to continue to originate and service assets effectively. It also serves as a useful barometer for investor feedback, as the syndicate team gauges the buildup of interest.

It should be noted that in some cases, an end investor has been identified early in the process (this may even be agreed on to be the issuer retaining the transaction).

Where the notes are to be issued to public investors however, the arranger will be tasked with pulling together material to facilitate the distribution of the notes. The material may also be vetted by the in-house legal team, particularly if selling into the United States where a number of disclosure requirements need to be met.

The marketing material may consist of the following:

- A red herring offering circular—a substantially finalized form of the prospectus to be made available to potential investors. The "red" will give investors a sound understanding of the transaction structure and mechanics and will also feature a detailed description of the assets and the portfolio composition. It won't feature pricing on the notes, as this will be finalized as part of the syndication process.
- A credit rating agency presale report (in some instances, and typically not if sold into the United States).
  - Once a rating process is complete (and during the marketing phase— before pricing), an agency will post a report for the deal, probably together with a press release, on its web site. The report will provide its subscribers with a broad description of the transaction and detail the underlying collateral and the approach in applying its published criteria to the transaction.
  - In presale reports, credit rating agencies will point out that the ratings in the report are preliminary at that stage. The reality is that the arranger will not announce the transaction if there is an expectation of a change in the preliminary stages. Agencies are unable to finalize things because (1) the pricing is not confirmed and (2) at the point the red herring is available, in some instances, underlying transaction documents are still being finalized.
  - Following the close of the transaction, an updated and final report, referred to as a new issue report, will be made available.
- An investor presentation. A majority of the content for the investor presentation will be drawn from the presentation prepared for the rating agencies. It will provide a good overview of the market and the originator, with a focus on the originator's origination and underwriting policies.

A template for an agency presentation is provided at Exhibit 6.13.

PRICING, CLOSE, AND SETTLEMENT

Analyze Assets	Provide Data	Select Rating Agencies	Undertake Legal Due Diligence	Model the Transaction	Determine Capital Structure/ Trigger Levels

| 1 | 2 | 3 | 4 | 5 | 6 | 7 | 8 | 9 | 10 | 11 | 12 | 13 | 14 | 15 | 16 |

Select Arranger	Appoint Third Parties	Commence Rating Agency Presentation	Begin Drafting Documents	Set up SPV	Prepare Marketing Materials	Price, Close, and Settle Transaction

Following the conclusion of the marketing phase, investors willing to participate in the bond issuance will provide the syndicate team of the lead managers with an indication of their willingness to participate. As part of the marketing, investors would have been given a price guide for the bonds. Investors would be invited to submit an order size and the price level associated with that order.

Typically, such an order book is allowed to grow beyond the required level of issuance and then pricing is revised as the book is calibrated to provide for an optimal price at the required issuance level. Price is not the exclusive driver here, as the syndicate has given consideration to a number of other factors, including providing an appropriate minimum allocation in return for the credit work put in by investors. Issuers are also wary of squeezing the price too much, which could cause investor discontent leading to reduced participation for subsequent transactions.

Once the deal is priced, this is communicated to investors and credit rating agencies.

Together with pricing, agencies also will be provided with the final pool that will now be selected as they finalize their cash flow models and prepare to provide a final, definitive rating. The credit rating agency collateral analysis to date will have been done on provisional, often larger pools. As loans continue to amortize during the structuring process, a final pool cut for the transaction is typically a subset of earlier versions. The final pool cut will be sized to be as close as possible to the aggregate size of the notes being issued.

From an originator's perspective, this final selection of loans will be earmarked in the systems to be sold to the issuing vehicle. In jurisdictions where the local public registry has to be notified, lawyers will prepare the relevant information to ensure this registration process can take place on the morning of closing.

The registration process is one of a number of condition precedents (CPs) that would need to be satisfied on the morning of closing ahead of the actual settlement of the bonds. Other CPs include release of final rating letters from all rating agencies, execution of all transaction documents, and a bring-down call with the issuer. To minimize execution risk, every attempt will be made to get the letters and documents in place the day before and held in escrow.

Once CPs have all been met, the actual closing day settlement process can begin. The arranger will also likely take the role of interface between investors and the common depository. We have set out below an illustration of the movement of bonds and cash that would need to take place.

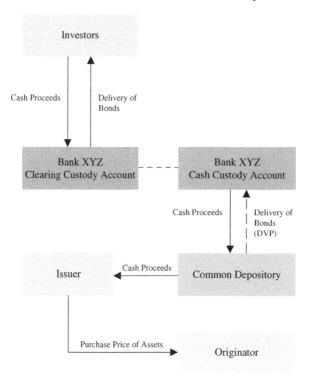

SUMMARY AND CONCLUSIONS

In Chapter 4 we have provided insight into some of the thoughts and processes behind the rating and legal aspects of a transaction. It should be mentioned here that this is where the greatest risk to the overall success of a transaction lies, and consequently, where there is greatest focus.

Law firms, rating agencies, and originators are all vested stakeholders, in addition to the arranger who will take overall responsibility for a structure and provide guidance based on analysis and past experience.

A stable rating for a transaction (post-closing) is vital and so it is essential for agencies to get their legal and asset analysis correct and consistent from the outset. In instances where this does not happen, the retreat is a very public one and there is a tangible risk of a subsequent impact on the market valuation for the affected security. The arranger, too, has to mitigate this by presenting a structure that can stand the test of time. There is no point in putting a structure together that requires asset performance that cannot be sustained for the expected life of the deal.

Similarly, given the complexity of some structures and the potential for litigation and financial loss, the legal documentation has to be precise and comprehensive. This becomes even more of an issue as translations cross borders, with borrowers in several jurisdictions party to contracts under a number of governing laws. The consequence of an SPV not being able to enforce on an asset is likely to be severe. Recent events have shown that it is necessary to consider every eventuality, however remote.

..

CHAPTER 5

Static Synthetic CDO Cash Flow Waterfall Model

In this chapter we illustrate a working cash flow waterfall model for a hypothetical synthetic collateralized debt obligation (CDO), appropriately named "Synthetic CDO Ltd.," issue size $115 million. The object is to demonstrate how the cash flow waterfall would be laid out when modeled for the structuring of the deal.

The model describes a partially funded synthetic CDO, with a super-senior portfolio credit default swap (CDS) and tranched credit-linked notes (CLNs). The assets of the CDO are single-name CDS contracts that reference a portfolio of 100 corporate names. The proceeds of the CLN issue are invested in collateral securities of German bunds, which are then repo'd out to a repo counterparty and act as collateral for the CLN issue. The return on the collateral securities represents an element of credit protection for the CLN investors, who can expect a minimum return based on return on collateral. However, the excess return to CLN noteholders is made up of the credit-linked return, linked to the reference assets.

The definitions refer to a hypothetical offering circular (OC) for this transaction.

Exhibit 5.1 shows the note tranching of this transaction and a summary of deal terms and static data.

The waterfall itself is shown in Exhibit 5.2. This describes the priority of payments, which is given by the note tranching described in Exhibit 5.1. Note that taxes and the fees of the vehicle, such as trustee fees, rank above the note liabilities. The spreadsheet would be used in conjunction with the offering circular (OC) for the transaction (not shown here). We reference at "A" where the value for the Class B-1 note interest distribution amount will fall: This amount is the payment of excess interest after the application of interest and principal payments of A3 and par coverage tests. The bottom half of the

EXHIBIT 5.1 Synthetic CDO Ltd. static data

Note Class	Price	Original Value	Period Start Principal Amount	Deferred Interest (b/f)	Principal Amount Adjusted for Intra Period Events*	Principal Reduction	Period End Principal Amount	Deferred Interest (c/f)	Denom. O/S (start)	Denom. O/S (end)	Interest per EUR 1k Note	Margin	Interest Due	Interest Paid
A-1	100%	38,250,000	38,250,000	-	38,250,000	-	38,250,000		50,000.00	50,000.00	441.73	0.0045	337,923.45	337,923.45
A-2	100%	21,250,000	21,250,000	-	21,250,000	-	21,250,000		50,000.00	50,000.00	467.01	0.0065	198,479.25	198,479.25
A-3	100%	29,750,000	29,750,000	-	29,750,000	-	29,750,000	-	50,000.00	50,000.00	587.08	0.0160	349,312.60	349,312.60
B-1	100%	20,400,000	10,656,875	-	10,656,875	-	2,985,625		26,119.79	7,317.71	-	-	-	-
B-2	100%	5,100,000	-	-	-	-	-		0.00	0.00	-	-	-	-

*Cash Settlement Amounts & Deferred interest outstanding at such time

STATIC DATA

Closing Date	8/9/2002
Scheduled Maturity Redemption Date	8/9/2012
Final Payment Date	10/9/2013
Period Start Date	11/25/2002
Period End Date	2/24/2003
Period (days)	91
Pay Method	360
Three-Month Euribor	0.03045
Repurchase Date	Y
Maturity or Redemption Event	N
Repo Termination Event	N
Unsettled Credit Events	N
Denomination	50,000

EXHIBIT 5.2 Synthetic CDO Ltd. waterfall

SYNTHETIC CDO LTD.

INTEREST WATERFALL 1,650,413.23

	Due	Paid	Balance
Taxes, Registration owing by the Issuer	-	-	1,650,413.23
Trustee and Administrator Charges	9,015	9,015	1,641,398.44
Other Admin Expenses	46,640	46,640	1,594,758.00
Expense Account Top Up	-	-	1,594,758.00
Interest payments on Class A-1	337,923	337,923	1,256,834.55
Interest payments on Class A-2	198,479	198,479	1,058,355.30
Interest payments on Class A-3	349,313	349,313	709,042.70
Par Coverage	709,043	709,043	-
Class B-1 Interest Distribution Amount	-	-	-

PRINCIPAL WATERFALL

	Amounts Due	Paid	Balance
REVISED BALANCE ON PRINCIPAL PAYMENT DATE	-	-	-
(Int. on subordinate Notes)			
Unpaid Taxes, Registration owing by the Issuer	-	-	-
Unpaid Trustee and Administrator Charges	-	-	-
Unpaid Other Admin Charges	-	-	-
Unpaid Expense Account Top Up	-	-	-
Unpaid Interest payments on Class A-1	-	-	-
Principal payments on Class A-1	38,250,000	-	-
Unpaid Interest payments on Class A-2	-	-	-
Principal payments on Class A-2	21,250,000	-	-
Interest payments on Class A-3	-	-	-
Principal payments on Class A-3	29,750,000	-	-
Class A-3 Deferred interest	-	-	-
B-1Note Rate Interest	-	-	-
Principal payments on Class B-1	10,656,875	-	-
Principal payments on Class B-2	5,279,156	-	-

EXHIBIT 5.3 Model inputs

SYNTHETIC CDO LTD.

Inputs	Fees	Accounts	Events	Static Data	Note Amount O/S (b/f)	Credit Events	Terms
Static Data							
Period Start Date	11/25/2002						
Period End Date	2/24/2003						
Three-Month Euribor	0.03045			Refer definition p35 - Offering Circular*			
Events							
Maturity or Redemption Date	N						
Repo Termination Event	N			Refer definition p53 - Offering Circular*			
Unsettled Credit Events	N			A Credit Event Notice has been delivered wrt a Ref. Entity but the related Cash Sett. Amount has not yet been paid			
Aggregate Amount Outstanding (b/f)							
Class A-1 Note	38,250,000						
Class A-2 Note	21,250,000						
Class A-3 Note	29,750,000						
A-3 Notes Deferred Interest	-						
Class B-1 Note	10,656,875						
Class B-2 Note	-						
Accounts							
Collateral Account (24437301)				"Accounts": Refer p96 - Offering Circular*			
Opening Balance (bf)	31,717						
Net Proceeds of the Notes	99,906,875						
Market Value of the Repo Securities	105,027,176			MTM Weekly for De Minimis Test and Credit Swap Test			
Payment Account (24437303 - Balance at Pay Date)							
Opening Balance	-						

Expense Account (24437304)		
Opening Balance	60,640	
Unpaid Issuer Expenses	-	
Other Net Movements	-	
Collection Account (24437302)		
Opening Balance	95,768	
Fees		
Taxes, Registration owing by the Issuer		Taxes and filing fees and registration fees (including without limitation, annual return fees) owing by the Issuer
Trustee and Administrator Charges	9,015	Accrued and unpaid costs, charges, fees and expenses owing to the Trustee and Administrator
Other Admin Expenses	46,640	Accrued and unpaid Administrative expenses (other than fees described above)
Credit Events		
Aggregate of all Cash Settlement Amounts	14,843,125.00	The sum of all Cash Settlement Amounts paid to date (prior to Period start date)
Aggregate of all Reinstatement Amounts	-	The sum of all Reinstatement Amounts paid to date (prior to Period end date)
Cash Settlement Amounts	7,671,250.00	A cash payment the Issuer is obliged to make when a Credit Event occurs wrt a Reference Entity
Reinstatement Amounts	-	A refund on a Cash Settlement Amount paid, but determined to be incorrect in accordance to the Credit Swap
Terms		
Repurchased Securities: Originator to Provide Figures		
Initial Purchase Price	114,750,000.00	As per Repo Confirmation
Payment of Principal on the Notes to be Made		The purchase price at which the Issuer will purchase Eligible securities from the Repo Counterparty On a Repurchase Date
Agg. Collateral Account Replenishment Payment (to date)	653,476.05	Aggregate Repo Securities purchased to satisfy Par Coverage test
Aggregate Repurchase Price paid (to date)	22,514,375.00	Aggregate price value of Equivalent securities sold to the Repo Counterparty for Cash Settlement Payments
Repo Rate Payents Accrued and Unpaid	-	Refers Repo Rate Payments relating to Repurchase Dates occuring in interest period preceding this Payment Date . . . see below
Repo Rate Payments Paid	762,341.92	(equals Repo Rate Payments due on Payment Date and all other Repo Rate Payments made since the prior Payment Date)
Calculation Amount (for Unsettled Credit Events)	-	Refer definition p48 - Offering Circular*

(continued)

EXHIBIT 5.3 *(continued)*

SYNTHETIC CDO LTD.

Inputs	Fees	Accounts	Events	Static Data	Note Amount O/S (b/f)	Credit Events	Terms
Max Portfolio Notional Amount (p51)	841,500,000.00				Refer definition p51 - Offering Circular*		
Credit Swap Payment	792,303.19				The amount received by the Issuer under the Credit Swap		
Interest rec'd wrt to Securities Sold by Issuer	-				All accrued interest received in cash by the Issuer with respect to Securities sold by the Issuer		
Discount Payments (After Repo Term.)	-				If the Repo Agreement is no longer in place, all payments of interest (including the accreted portion of a discount) on - Repo Securities received in cash by the Issuer during such Interest Period		

Offering Circular dd 28 Sept 2002

spreadsheet shows the remaining calculations required for the junior note liabilities.

Exhibit 5.3 shows the inputs to the model. These are given by the terms in the OC, and include the detailed calculations for each cash flow item. The results are given in Exhibit 5.4, which is essentially the model output. We see at the bottom that there are sufficient funds in the vehicle to pay down the waterfall cash settlement account. The figure shows receipts of cash to the vehicle beginning with note proceeds on issue and then subsequent items such as repo interest. It also shows results of the par coverage test, which shows if the vehicle has sufficient cash to cover liabilities at par, as well as cash flows resulting from credit events of any assets in the portfolio. These are marked "A" and "B" on the spreadsheet.

Finally, Exhibit 5.5 is a summary of the bank accounts associated with the structure. It shows the cash flow movements in the vehicle's bank accounts at the time the calculation is made on the model.

SUMMARY AND CONCLUSIONS

This chapter illustrated what a working cash flow model for an asset-backed security or CDO deal might look like. The model is developed as part of the capital structure and tranching process undertaken during the securitization process, which was described in Chapter 4.

EXHIBIT 5.4   Model output

SYNTHETIC CDO LTD.

PURCHASED SECURITIES

REPURCHASE PRICE	7,671,250
OUTSTANDING PURCHASE PRICE	92,889,101
REMAINING PURCHASE PRICE	100,560,351
Cash settlement amount	7,671,250
Payment of principal on the notes to be made	-
Initial purchase price	114,750,000
Collateral account replenishment payments	709,043
Repo rate payments accrued and unpaid	-
Repo rate payments paid	762,342
Aggregate of collateral account replenishment amts paid	653,476
Aggregate of repurchase prices paid	22,514,375

(continued)

EXHIBIT 5.4   *(continued)*

TERMS

Issuance of notes proceeds	114,750,000
Excess repo securities	-
Calculation amount (for unsettled credit events)	-
Max portfolio notional amount	841,500,000
Credit swap payment	792,303
Collateral account investment income	762,342
Interest rec'd wrt to securities sold by issuer	-
Repo rate payment	762,342
Discount payments (after repo term.)	-

(A) PAR COVERAGE

Ratio (at period start)	1.040774241
Value	1.11
Test	FAIL
10/1/2003	1.11
10/1/2004	0
Thereafter	0

PURCHASED SECURITIES

Reviewed Weekly

Applicable percentage	1.03	
Required amount		88,288,743
De minimis amount		214,293
Condition	**MARGIN SURPLUS**	
		TRUE

(B) CREDIT EVENTS

Aggregate of all cash settlement amounts	14,843,125
Aggregate of all reinstatement amounts	-
Cash settlement amounts	7,671,250
Reinstatement amounts	-

SUFFICIENT FUNDS TO PAY CASH SETTLEMENT AMOUNT

EXHIBIT 5.5 Vehicle bank accounts

SYNTHETIC CDO LTD.

COLLATERAL ACCOUNT

Opening Balance (bf)	31,716.84
Net Proceeds of the Notes	99,906,875.00
Repo Securities (Market Value)	105,027,176
Replenishment Payment	709,043
Principal Amortization Payment (c/f)	-
B-2 Note Principal Balance Adjustment	-
Reinstatement Amounts	-
Cash Settlement Amount	7,671,250
Closing Balance	198,003,561

PAYMENT ACCOUNT (BALANCE AT PAY DATE)

Opening Balance	-
Transfer from Collection Account	1,650,413
Waterfall Payments	1,650,413
Revenue	1,650,413
Principal	-
Excess Repo Securities	-
Closing Balance	-

EXPENSE ACCOUNT

Opening Balance	60,640
Movements	-
Condition as per O.C.	-
Unpaid Issuer Expenses	-
Other Net Movements	0
Closing Balance*	60,640

COLLECTION ACCOUNT

Opening Balance	95,768.12
Credit Swap Receipts	792,303.19
Collateral Investment Income	762,341.92
Interest rec'd wrt to Securities sold by Issuer	-
Repo Receipts	762,341.92
Discount Payments (after repo term.)	-
Transfer Balance to Payment Account	1,650,413.23
Closing Balance	-

*On final principal pay date, balance transferred to payment account.

PART
Three

Transaction Closing Templates and Checklists

In Part Three we provide a series of templates that could be employed by an originator when structuring and closing a conventional ABS or CLO transaction. They can be applied to most such deals, and are designed to help enable a first-time originator to set up the required processes immediately. The templates provided here hold data from an actual transaction, "Red Sea Funding Limited," which helps to illustrate how the templates would be used in practice.

We also provide detail on the rating agency review and legal review process, again through the use of templates and checklists.

CHAPTER **6**

Transaction Templates and Checklists

This chapter includes a series of example templates, checklists, and pro forma to illustrate the process of structuring a typical loans asset-backed security (ABS) or collateralized loan obligation (CLO) transaction. The examples shown are live working documents and worksheets, and so should be applicable to most deals. The intention is that they are of value to practitioners looking to close an ABS, particularly first-time originators.

The exhibits presented here are specific to the Red Sea Corporate Loans ABS transaction closed by Europe Arab Bank (EAB) in 2009. This was an in-house securitization that was arranged to generate collateral for use at the European Central Bank, and all the issued liabilities were bought by the originator. However, as a transaction it illustrated every aspect of the work of a conventional externally placed ABS or CLO, from the rating process to the legal review and engagement of third-party suppliers. The forms can be considered generic for any cash flow ABS transaction, and are applicable to any financial institution. We recommend them to first-time originators contemplating closing their first ABS deal.

RED SEA MASTER SERIES LIMITED STRUCTURE DIAGRAM

Exhibit 6.1 shows the final transaction structure diagram, including the SPV structure and tranched liabilities. As a transaction, Red Sea was unusual in that it had a multi-SPV set up. This was to enable the multicurrency nature of it to be handled better from an operational viewpoint.

UNDERLYING ASSET POOL

Exhibit 6.2 is the full list of all the underlying corporate loans securitized into the SPV, with the detail of loan size, type, interest basis, and other relevant

113

EXHIBIT 6.1 Red Sea Master Series Limited structure diagram

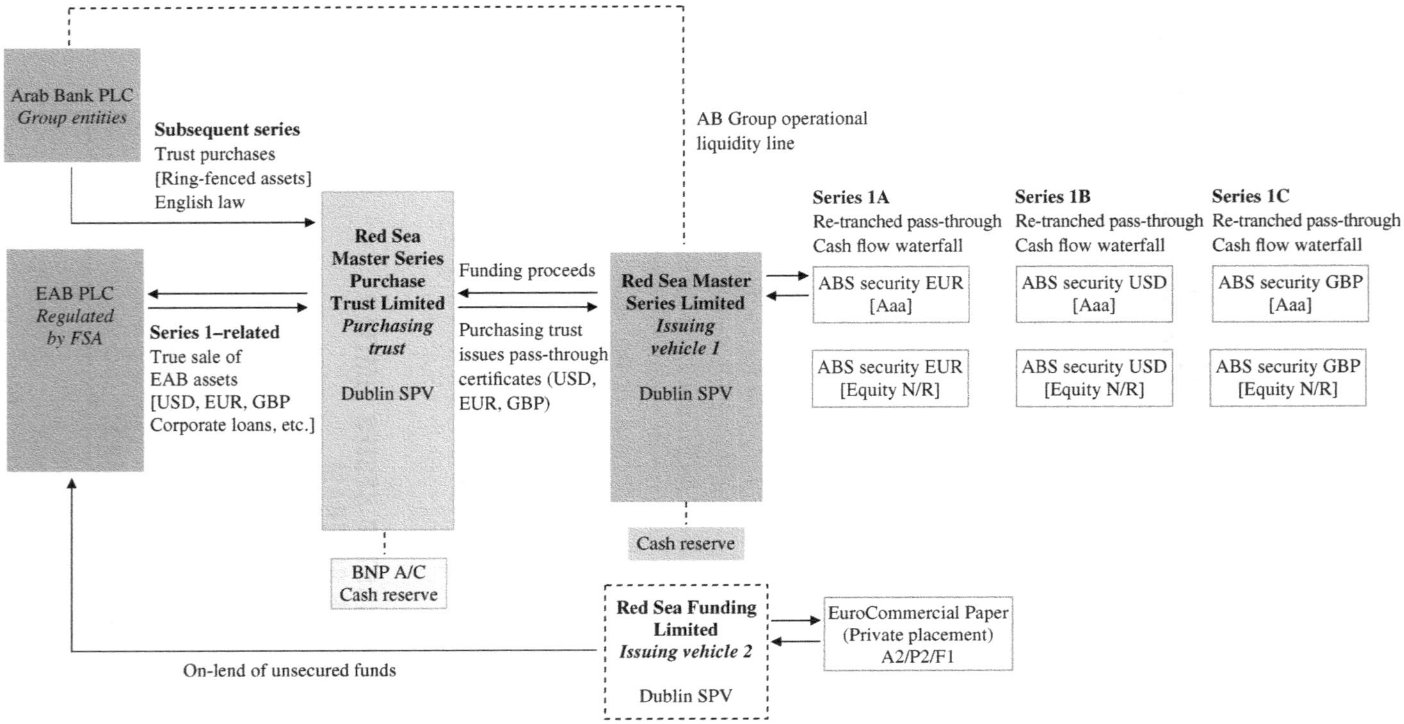

EXHIBIT 6.2 Full list of underlying asset pool

Loan Name	Sector	Loan Type	Currency	Total Original Balance	Total Current Balance	Issue Date	Maturity Date	Coupon Type	Benchmark	Interest Basis	Int Freq Code
AES BARKA S.A.O.C.	Elec, gas, steam & hot water	SYNDICATED LOANS FIXED	USD	382,000,000		30-Oct-03	27-Apr-17	Floating	1YR USD LIBOR	ACT/360	Yearly, in Oct
FRESHWINDS FINANCE LIMITED	Letting of own property	DIRECT LOANS FIXED	GBP	2,250,000	2,250,000	27-Jul-07	27-Jul-12	Floating	3M GBP LIBOR	ACT/365	Quarterly, in Jan + Apr + Jul + Oct
EMIRATES CMS POWER COMPANY	Elec, gas, steam & hot water	SYNDICATED LOANS FIXED	USD	391,000,000		31-Mar-04	30-Jun-20	Floating	1YR USD LIBOR	ACT/360	Yearly, in Dec
EL BEHERA NATURAL GAS LIQEF CO SAE	Elec, gas, steam & hot water	SYNDICATED LOANS FIXED	USD	944,000,000		15-Dec-04	17-Dec-18	Floating	1M USD LIBOR	ACT/360	Monthly
SEMBCORP UTILITIES (UK) LIMITED	Electricity, prod. & distr.	SYNDICATED LOANS FIXED	GBP	116,000,000		25-Apr-05	30-Dec-16	Floating	6M GBP LIBOR	ACT/365	Half yearly, in Jun + Dec
IDKU NATURAL GAS LIQUEFACTION CO	Extraction of crude petroleum	SYNDICATED LOANS FIXED	USD	760,000,000		15-Dec-05	15-Dec-16	Floating	1M USD LIBOR	ACT/360	Monthly
ABC INTERNATIONAL RE OBU BAHRAIN	Financial Intermediation	SYNDICATED LOANS FIXED	USD	5,000,000	5,000,000	30-Mar-06	24-Mar-11	Floating	3M USD LIBOR	ACT/360	Quarterly, in Jan + Apr + Jul + Oct
SIDI KRIR GENERATING COMPANY	Electricity, prod. & distr.	SYNDICATED LOANS FIXED	USD	290,500,000		26-Jan-07	31-Oct-21	Floating	1YR USD LIBOR	ACT/360	Yearly, in Oct
SEMBCORP UTILITIES (UK) LIMITED	Electricity, prod. & distr.	SYNDICATED LOANS FIXED	GBP	116,000,000		29-Jun-07	30-Dec-16	Floating	3M GBP LIBOR	ACT/365	Quarterly, in Jan + Apr + Jul + Oct

(continued)

EXHIBIT 6.2 (continued)

Loan Name	Sector	Loan Type	Currency	Total Original Balance	Total Current Balance	Issue Date	Maturity Date	Coupon Type	Benchmark	Interest Basis	Int Freq Code
CITY INN LTD	Hotels & restaurants	SYNDICATED LOANS FIXED	GBP	121,500,000	159,000,000	30-Mar-07	30-Mar-12	Floating	3M GBP LIBOR	ACT/365	Quarterly, in Mar + Jun + Sep + Dec
ENRC MARKETING AG	Manuf basic metals	SYNDICATED LOANS FIXED	USD	1,480,000,000	577,564,606	17-Mar-08	20-Apr-12	Floating	3M USD LIBOR	ACT/360	Quarterly, in Feb + May + Aug + Nov
JACKS PROPERTY LIMITED	Letting of own property	DIRECT LOANS FIXED	GBP	2,130,000	2,130,000	30-May-07	30-Apr-12	Floating	3M GBP LIBOR	ACT/365	Quarterly, in Feb + May + Aug + Nov
AES ENERGIA CARTAGENA	Elec, gas, steam & hot water	SYNDICATED LOANS FIXED	EUR	742,000,000		6-Aug-07	30-Dec-27	Floating	3M EURIBOR	ACT/360	Quarterly, in Mar + Jun + Sep + Dec
SPANISH EGYPTIAN GAS COMPANY SAE	Extraction of crude petroleum	SYNDICATED LOANS FIXED	USD	720,000,000	619,464,142	15-Sep-08	15-Sep-22	Floating	1YR USD LIBOR	ACT/360	Yearly, in Sep
AJMAN SEWERAGE (PRIVATE)LTD COMPANY	Collection, purification	SYNDICATED LOANS FIXED	USD	100,000,000		6-Sep-07	12-Jan-26	Floating	1YR USD LIBOR	ACT/360	Yearly, in Sep
SABIC INNOVATIVE PLASTICS B.V.	Manuf chemical products	SYNDICATED LOANS FIXED	EUR	6,600,000,000	5,745,000,000	6-Sep-07	29-Aug-14	Floating	3M EURIBOR	ACT/360	Quarterly, in Jan + Apr + Jul + Oct
CANYON MELEZIN S.A.S	Hotels	DIRECT LOANS FIXED	EUR	20,000,000	20,000,000	7-Sep-07	7-Sep-12	Floating	6M EURIBOR	ACT/360	Half yearly, in Mar + Sep
SOHAR ALUMINIUM COMPANY	MaFct basic precious and other	SYNDICATED LOANS FIXED	USD	1,200,000,000	1,200,000,000	30-Nov-07	31-May-21	Floating	1YR USD LIBOR	ACT/360	Yearly, in Nov
TATA STEEL NETHERLANDS B.V	Manuf basic metals	SYNDICATED LOANS FIXED	EUR	1,590,000,000	1,182,996,974	21-Dec-07	28-Sep-12	Floating	3M EURIBOR	ACT/360	Quarterly, in Mar + Jun + Sep + Dec

EXHIBIT 6.2 (*continued*)

Loan Name	Sector	Loan Type	Currency	Total Original Balance	Total Current Balance	Issue Date	Maturity Date	Coupon Type	Benchmark	Interest Basis	Int Freq Code
25 NORTH COLONNADE INVESTMT CO LTD	Real estate activities	SYNDICATED LOANS FIXED	GBP	205,750,000	205,750,000	1-Nov-07	18-Oct-13	Floating	6M GBP LIBOR	ACT/365	Half yearly, in Apr + Oct
AUTOBAHN TANK & RAST HOLDINGS GMBH	Letting of own property	SYNDICATED LOANS FIXED	EUR	1,800,000,000	1,800,000,000	9-Nov-07	17-Oct-14	Floating	1YR EURIBOR	ACT/360	Yearly, in Dec
BRUSSELS AIRPORT HOLDING CO SA	Air transport	SYNDICATED LOANS FIXED	EUR	1,636,000,000		12-Nov-07	31-Dec-12	Floating	3M EURIBOR	ACT/360	Quarterly, in Jan + Apr + Jul + Oct
TRAFIGURA BEHEER B.V.ASIA	Wholesale on a fee or contract	SYNDICATED LOANS FIXED	USD	700,000,000	700,000,000	20-Nov-07	15-Nov-12	Floating	3M USD LIBOR	ACT/360	Quarterly, in Jan + Apr + Jul + Oct
SOVEREIGN HOTELS LTD	Hotels	DIRECT LOANS FIXED	EUR	45,000,000	45,000,000	4-Dec-07	30-Nov-12	Floating	3M EURIBOR	ACT/360	Quarterly, in Mar + Jun + Sep + Dec
HOLDINGS LES AIRELLES SAS	Hotels	SYNDICATED LOANS FIXED	EUR	65,094,356	62,872,425	17-Dec-07	12-May-14	Floating	1YR EURIBOR	ACT/360	Yearly, in Nov
HOTEL LES AIRELLES SAS	Hotels	SYNDICATED LOANS FIXED	EUR	1,016,365	16,745,000	18-Feb-08	12-May-14	Floating	6M EURIBOR	ACT/360	Half yearly, in Mar + Sep
W2005/THIRTY-FOUR B.V	Hotels	SYNDICATED LOANS FIXED	EUR	364,000,000	364,000,000	18-Oct-08	18-Oct-10	Floating	3M EURIBOR	ACT/360	Quarterly, in Jan + Apr + Jul + Oct
KUWAIT FOREIGN PETROLEUM EXPLORATIO	Extraction of crude petroleum	SYNDICATED LOANS FIXED	USD	320,000,000	320,000,000	19-May-08	10-May-13	Floating	3M USD LIBOR	ACT/360	Quarterly, in Feb + May + Aug + Nov
AIR FRANCE	Air transport	SYNDICATED LOANS FLOATING	EUR	78,546,364	43,252,316	21-Mar-07	20-Mar-15	Floating	1YR EURIBOR	ACT/360	Yearly, in Sep

(continued)

EXHIBIT 6.2 (continued)

Loan Name	Sector	Loan Type	Currency	Total Original Balance	Total Current Balance	Issue Date	Maturity Date	Coupon Type	Benchmark	Interest Basis	Int Freq Code
ORASCOM TELECOM TUNISIE	Telecommunications	SYNDICATED LOANS FLOATING	EUR	225,000,000	82,874,901	23-Jun-06	31-Mar-11	Floating	3M EURIBOR	ACT/360	Quarterly, in Mar + Jun + Sep + Dec
ENT.TUNISIENNE ACTIVITES PETROLIERE	Extraction of petroleum/gas	SYNDICATED LOANS FLOATING	USD	150,000,000	90,000,000	16-Apr-07	4-Apr-12	Floating	1YR USD LIBOR	ACT/360	Yearly, in Oct
OMAN INDIA FERTILISER COMPANY S.A.O	Manufacture of basic chemicals	SYNDICATED LOANS FIXED	USD	592,000,000		14-Jan-08	15-Jul-15	Floating	6M USD LIBOR	ACT/360	Half yearly, in Jan + Jul
DASMAN LTD	Air transport	SYNDICATED LOANS FIXED	USD	45,000,000	28,841,485	1-Jul-04	12-Apr-13	Floating	3M USD LIBOR	ACT/360	Quarterly, in Jan + Apr + Jul + Oct
ALJAHRA LTD	Air transport	SYNDICATED LOANS FLOATING	USD	33,500,000	28,330,804	24-Oct-06	24-Jan-13	Floating	3M USD LIBOR	ACT/360	Quarterly, in Jan + Apr + Jul + Oct
ROSKO LEASE	Air transport	SYNDICATED LOANS FLOATING	EUR	13,500,000	3,979,481	3-Mar-99	3-Mar-11	Floating	6M EURIBOR	ACT/360	Half yearly, in Mar + Sep
EIFFARIE SAS	Other supporting transport act	SYNDICATED LOANS FLOATING	EUR	5,850,000,000	5,655,439,520	3-May-07	28-Feb-13	Floating	1YR EURIBOR	ACT/360	Yearly, in Dec
SNC UM AMAD LEASING (QATAR AIRWAYS)	Air transport	SYNDICATED LOANS FLOATING	EUR	78,002,619	72,685,106	18-Jun-08	19-Dec-22	Floating	3M EURIBOR	ACT/360	Quarterly, in Mar + Jun + Sep + Dec
BOURBON OFFSHORE GULF WLL	Water transport	SYNDICATED LOANS FLOATING	USD	12,375,000	10,828,125	22-May-08	22-Feb-18	Floating	6M USD LIBOR	ACT/360	Half yearly, in Feb + Aug
	Air transport		USD	120,560,475	116,417,158	26-Nov-08	26-Nov-14	Floating		ACT/360	

EXHIBIT 6.2 (*continued*)

Loan Name	Sector	Loan Type	Currency	Total Original Balance	Total Current Balance	Issue Date	Maturity Date	Coupon Type	Benchmark	Interest Basis	Int Freq Code
LAHWAYLA LEASING LIMITED (QATAR AIR)		SYNDICATED LOANS FLOATING							1YR USD LIBOR		Yearly, in Nov
CHATEAU HOTEL MONT ROYAL SAS	Hotels & restaurants	DIRECT LOANS FLOATING	EUR	14,000,000	14,000,000	10-Oct-08	10-Oct-13	Floating	6M EURIBOR	ACT/360	Half yearly, in Apr + Oct
OMAN INDIA FERTILISER COMPANY S.A.O	Manufacture of basic chemicals	SYNDICATED LOANS FIXED	USD	592,000,000		17-Jul-06	17-Jul-15	Floating	1YR USD LIBOR	ACT/360	Yearly, in Nov
BARILLA HOLDING S.P.A.	Manufacture of other food prod	SYNDICATED LOANS FIXED	EUR	1,500,000,000	1,750,000,000	3-Aug-07	31-Jul-12	Floating	3M EURIBOR	ACT/360	Quarterly, in Feb + May + Aug + Nov
ABENGOA S.A.	Building installation	SYNDICATED LOANS FIXED	EUR	300,000,000	300,000,000	23-Jan-07	20-Jul-12	Floating	3M EURIBOR	ACT/360	Quarterly, in Jan + Apr + Jul + Oct
BEFESA ZINC S.L.	Recycling of metal waste	SYNDICATED LOANS FIXED	EUR	355,500,000	287,244,000	27-Apr-07	27-Oct-13	Floating	1M EURIBOR	ACT/360	Monthly
ACS ACTIVIDADES DE CONSTRUCCION SER	Building of constructions	SYNDICATED LOANS FIXED	EUR	1,500,000,000	1,500,000,000	23-Jul-07	19-Jul-12	Floating	1M EURIBOR	ACT/360	Monthly
DHOFAR POWER COMPANY SAOG	Elec, gas, steam & hot water	SYNDICATED LOANS FIXED	USD	340,000,000		4-Sep-07	30-Apr-18	Floating	6M USD LIBOR	ACT/360	Half yearly, in May + Nov
OILTANKING FINANCE B.V.	Supporting/ auxill transport	SYNDICATED LOANS FIXED	EUR	80,000,000	80,000,000	16-Dec-05	16-Dec-10	Floating	1YR EURIBOR	ACT/365 /366	Yearly, in Dec
STADA ARZNEIMITTEL AG	Mafct pharm, med chemical & biological	SYNDICATED LOANS FIXED	EUR	40,000,000	40,000,000	9-Aug-06	9-Aug-10	Floating	1YR EURIBOR	ACT/ 365/366	Yearly, in Aug

details. Note that in some cases the loan notional at time of the transaction was below the original loan size; this denotes a facility that is amortizing, with some of the balance paid down.

DRAFT TERM SHEET

Exhibit 6.3 is a reproduction of the initial term sheet used when originating the transaction, which is updated during the due diligence process and used as part of the rating agency presentation. It is issued as final on deal closing.

EXHIBIT 6.3 Draft term sheet

Red Sea Master Series Limited
EUR 1 billion corporate loans Master Series Trust asset-backed liabilities
Indicative Terms and Conditions
xxx xxx 2009

Capital Structure

Class	Size	Currency	Type	Rating	Legal Final	Coupon
A1	[ ]	EUR	FRN	Aaa	xxx 2030	3m Euribor + 40 bps
A2	[ ]	USD	FRN	Aaa	xxx 2030	3m Libor + 40 bps
A3	[ ]	GBP	FRN	Aaa	xxx 2030	3m Libor + 40 bps
B1	[ ]	EUR	FRN	Baa2	xxx 2030	3m Euribor + 70 bps
B2	[ ]	USD	FRN	Baa2	xxx 2030	3m Libor + 70 bps
C1	[ ]	EUR	Equity	N/R	xxx 2030	Excess spread
C2	[ ]	USD	Equity	N/R	xxx 2030	Excess spread
C3	[ ]	GBP	Equity	N/R	xxx 2030	Excess spread

Issuer	Red Sea Master Series Limited, a special purpose company (SPV) incorporated with limited liability in Ireland
Arranger	Europe Arab Bank PLC
Listing	Irish Stock Exchange

EXHIBIT 6.3 *(continued)*

Reference Portfolio Summary	
Original reference portfolio	EUR 1,876,066,302
Current portfolio drawn balance	EUR 1,290,312,416
Committed headroom	EUR 585,753,876
Number of loans	222
Number of obligors	121
Average loan balance	EUR 5,812,218
Largest loan balance	EUR 48,580,875
Smallest loan balance	EUR 252,601
Category breakdown	SME (7%), Large corporate (93%)
Largest obligor	3.77%
Repayment profile breakdown	Fixed (%), Bullet (%), Variable (%)
Shortest loan maturity	27 February 2009
Longest loan maturity	30 April 2029
Average maturity	7.1 years
Number of loans collateralized	35 (20.9%)
Weighted-average spread	118.9 bps
Weighted-average rating	BBB+
Weighted-average interest rate margin	x bps
Percentage of loans senior	[ ] %

(continued)

EXHIBIT 6.3 (continued)

Structure Diagram

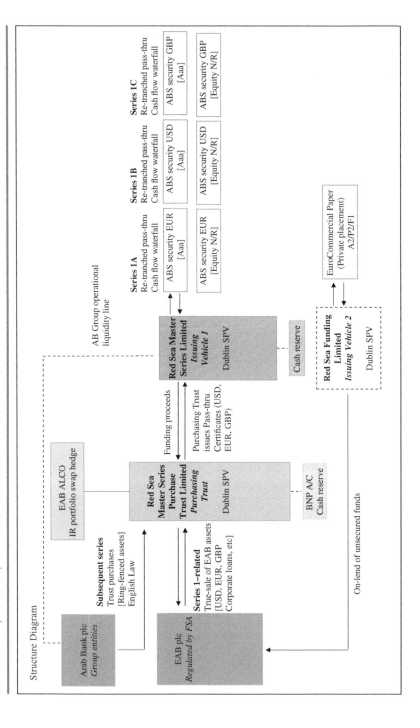

EXHIBIT 6.3 *(continued)*

Structure Diagram	
Timing	Cut-off date xxx 2008
	Pricing date n/a
	Final OC xxx 2009
	Settlement xxx 2009
Issue price	Par
Interest basis	Quarterly
Redemption	100% of the principal amount payable on the maturity date
Business days	London, TARGET
Lender of record	Europe Arab Bank PLC
Servicer	Europe Arab Bank PLC
Interest-rate swap counterparty	Europe Arab Bank PLC
Rating agency	Moody's
Clearance/Settlement	Euroclear, Clearstream
Liquidity backing	Operational liquidity backing of coupon payment dates by Arab Bank PLC
Liquidity line provider	N/A
Investor reporting	Issuer will produce monthly investor report for circulation to investors and other relevant third parties. Report will be distributed by the sub-administrator.
Fees	The fees of the issuer are payable by Europe Arab Bank PLC
Legal advisor	Orrick, Herrington & Sutcliffe
Irish counsel	Mattheson Ormsby Prentice
Trustee	TBC
Issuing and paying agent	TBC
Administrator	Europe Arab Bank PLC
Sub-administrator	TBC
Calculation agent	TBC
Issuer account bank	TBC
Custodian	Europe Arab Bank PLC
Corporate services	Ogier Corporate Services (Ireland) Ltd.
SPV administrator	Ogier Corporate Services (Ireland) Ltd.
Listing agent	NCB Stockbrokers
Irish paying agent	N/A
Auditor	Deloitte & Touche
Governing law	English

EXHIBIT 6.3 (*continued*)

ISIN	To be advised at each issuance on the final terms/pricing supplement	
Selected eligibility criteria	All loans performing USD, EUR, and GBP underlying Internal rating BBB-/Baa3 or higher Minimum maturity 6 months Maximum maturity 15 years	
Industry breakdown	Crude oil & natural gas	1.65%
	Food products & beverages	1.68%
	Chemicals & chemical products	3.47%
	Rubber & plastic products	2.13%
	Nonmetallic & mineral products	3.30%
	Basic metals, e.g., iron, steel	3.53%
	Machinery; engineering	0.23%
	Medical, precision & optical instruments	0.19%
	Transport equipment, e.g., ships, aircraft	0.38%
	Recycling, including scrap metal	3.63%
	Electricity, gas, steam & hot water supply	13.37%
	Construction: houses, buildings, roads	6.87%
	Wholesale trade & commercial trade	2.52%
	Hotels, restaurants, catering	16.79%
	Water transport; ferries, shipping, freight & cargo transport	0.09%
	Air transport; scheduled & nonscheduled flights	3.07%
	Cargo handling, storage & warehousing, travel agencies	1.35%
	Financial services (not insurance & pension funds): banks	18.91%
	Real estate & property; estate agency, etc.	8.53%
	Renting of machinery & equipment	0.20%
	Public administration & defense; Social Security, etc.	2.71%
	Sewage & refuse disposal	2.46%
	Sporting & cultural activities	2.93%

EXHIBIT 6.3 *(continued)*

Geographic breakdown	BAHRAIN	0.2%
	BELGIUM	2.6%
	BRITISH VIRGIN ISL	3.2%
	CANADA	0.2%
	EGYPT	0.8%
	FRANCE	13.4%
	GERMAN-FED REP	7.2%
	GREECE	0.1%
	ITALY	1.4%
	JERSEY, C.I.	2.9%
	JORDAN	0.7%
	KUWAIT	1.3%
	MOROCCO	0.2%
	NETHERLANDS	1.8%
	OMAN SULTANATE	6.9%
	OTHER U.A.E.	7.8%
	QATAR	1.8%
	RUSSIAN FEDERATION	0.5%
	SAUDI ARABIA	4.9%
	SPAIN	6.2%
	SWITZERLAND	1.9%
	TUNISIA	0.8%
	TURKEY	1.1%
	UNITED KINGDOM	29.7%
	UNITED STATES	2.5%

CLOSING PROCESS

Exhibit 6.4 is a vital template for every originator—particularly a first-time originator—and shows the checklist of the process used when the transaction is closed.

EXHIBIT 6.4   Closing process checklist

Red Sea Funding Limited
EUR 1 billion corporate loans Master Series Trust asset-backed liabilities
Indicative Terms and Conditions
20 April 2009
Closing Process

The closing process is based on the draft term sheet and structure diagram already circulated and is subject to modification. Detail alterations to the proposed structure will be made during the closing process as required for operational, legal, finance, tax, or other reasons.

Work already complete
Draft term sheet and description of structure
Initial discussion with rating agencies and legal counsel

Stage 1: 1–3 months
Engage and mandate third parties
- Legal counsel
- Rating agencies
- Issuing and paying agent
- Trustee
- Sub-administrator
- Identify SPV location
- Irish tax advisor
- SPV administrator
- Auditor

Drafting program documentation
- Initial draft by legal counsel
- Program OC, trustee agreement, etc.
- Submit to rating agencies, trustee
- Documentation updating is ongoing

Asset pool due diligence
- Review of legal framework

EXHIBIT 6.4 (*continued*)

- Line-by-line identification of eligible assets following criteria screening
- Cash flow modeling and capital calculations, etc.

Stage 2: 1 month
Clear taxation issues
Incorporate SPV
- Instruct SPV administrator

Stage 3: 1–3 months
EAB internal process sign-off
- NBF meeting
- Back office and middle office, Risk Management, Finance, Operations, Legal
- Technology, system testing for booking process
- Operations: confirming new processes for loan servicing, etc.

Rating agency presentation (Moody's) on site
IPA and trustee prepare for closing
- Bank accounts, settlement procedures, etc.

Instruct Irish Stock Exchange listing
- Listing agent

Arab Bank PLC documentation executed (liquidity of coupon payment mechanism)

Stage 4: 1 month
Confirm rating agency report (pre-close report)
Closing conference calls
- Third parties
- External counsel coordination

Close vehicle and close transaction
- EAB purchases SPV liabilities
- SPV purchases EAB assets via purchase trust

STRUCTURING NOTES

The following is a typical bank internal document that is a checklist of the type of issues that the rating agency will consider, and notes to retain when structuring the transaction. This will necessarily differ to suit the nuances of an individual transaction; we illustrate the basic principles in Exhibit 6.5.

EXHIBIT 6.5   Example of structuring notes

The Process

1. Prepare all the hard data in advance. Do all the due diligence ahead of the review. This includes historical data plus dynamic and static data. NOTE: The deal docs should follow the loan-level data.
2. Will need to go through bank's internal ratings process...evidence that it works (e.g., we put something on watch, it then goes bust), a dynamic process of reviewing the methodology. Rating agencies will take this data and give it a mapping.
3. Treasury will review the PowerPoint when it's ready. The whole team needs to do a dry run going through the review before the actual event. Take a whole day to prepare.

Structuring Questions

1. Revolver loans: Securitize the full notional amount and the spare cash held on reserve account. Items to check: (1) the legal treatment (2) is the loan secured by collateral. The process is (1) for a 10mm loan, with 6mm currently drawn (2) buy the full 10mm from EAB, pay 6mm to EAB and hold the 4mm on Red Sea account. As it's drawn, Red Sea pays out to borrower
2. Paydown of loans: Word the deal so that if there is any paydown of loans, partial or full, Red Sea has right to purchase a replacement asset from EAB. There is no need to put the loan back to EAB: Use paydown proceeds to buy the new asset. This facility will require a revolving period during which Red Sea can buy the new loan.
3. This process means the overlying note (plus pass-through) does not need to be paid down. The rating agency must be comfortable that there will be no deterioration of the portfolio. Will need to convince the agency that dynamics of portfolio are safe.
4. Replacement loan should be purchased on a coupon date (IPD) and must pass CDO-ROM test.
5. Set the clause in docs that says any paydown can be held to next ABS coupon date, cash held on account until then (or used to purchase assets).
6. Red Sea can set the revolving period time scale: This will be a maximum period during which replacement asset can be purchased. This should be 1 or 2 years.

Waterfall Model

1. Set up a simple assets and liabilities cash flow model. That will suffice.

RATING AGENCY PREPARATION AND QUESTIONNAIRE

Exhibit 6.6 is a comprehensive checklist of all the issues and data require-ments that are considered as part of the rating agency review process. It is in several parts, including a rating agency questionnaire for corporate loans securitization and a checklist of the loan-level data required in advance by the rating agency.

This also illustrates the volume of data required when securitizing a deal, and we note its comprehensive nature. A bank may need to undertake considerable due diligence of the target assets on its balance sheet before it can send the required details to the rating agency. This is because the data may not be available in the format required, in which case the bank will need to conduct a line-by-line review of every loan in the pool it is looking to securitize. This process is known as asset enablement— the steps taken to "enable" the assets so that they are ready to be securitized. The checklist is a useful guide on what level of loan-level data is required.

EXHIBIT 6.6 Rating agency preparation and questionnaire

I. Industry Perspective

Market

1. How old is the company loan market?
2. How large is the company loan market?
3. Describe the general trends in the company loan market over the past 5 to 10 years.
4. What form of security is taken over the loans?
5. Please describe the segments of the market (small business loans, medium-size company loans, corporate loans . . .)

Products

1. Explain the historical and current characteristics of company loans.
2. Discuss reasons for any changes in loan products over time.
3. What is the average deposit for loan holders?
4. What is/are the typical repayment method(s)?
5. Were/are the interest rates fixed or floating? What percentage of market is this? If floating, how often were/are rates changed? Was/is interest capitalized?

(continued)

EXHIBIT 6.6 (*continued*)

6. What is the typical maturity of a loan?
7. On what was/is the company loan interest rate based? How, if at all, has this changed with time?
8. To date, what have been the highest rates of interest? When did these peaks occur? How did they impact on the market, in terms of loan payments, prepayments, defaults, and foreclosures? Please provide details on movements in rates.
9. What were/are the sources of funding for company loan lending?
10. Please describe the different facilities provided: loans, leasing, factoring, lines of credit, and so forth.

Participants

1. Historically and currently, who were/are the providers of company loans?
2. Are there more lenders entering the market now? If so, why?
3. What is the difference among the lenders and their products?
4. Who are the current lenders? Explain their competitive position with respect to portfolio size and market share.
5. Is there a specific client profile for different types of lenders? Would a borrower have an existing customer relationship with its lender?

II. Origination/Servicing

General Company Information

1. Company overview and history
2. Strategy and goals of organization
3. Financial position
4. Structure of organization
5. Management depth and experience
6. Number of employees per department
7. Business volume: past/present/anticipated
8. Strategic importance of the company finance business
9. Rationale for securitization: Is the transaction a one-off or part of a planned series of deals?

Sources of Origination

1. Dealer network
2. Branch network

EXHIBIT 6.6 *(continued)*

---

3. Direct mail
4. Advertising
5. Other

Marketing Strategy

1. Pricing: Determination, frequency and distribution
2. Geographic region: Growth areas
3. Loan products: Plans for new products
4. Customer base
5. Internet usage

Underwriting Process and Criteria

1. Development of credit policy, future strategy
2. Underwriting criteria and key parameters
3. Approval mechanisms and processes, controls, checks, and delegation
4. Preapprovals and overrides
5. Approval/decline rates and reasons
6. Verification procedures
7. Monitoring and control
8. Historical application volume and processing time
9. Historical funding and efficiency ratios
10. Retention strategies
11. Evaluation and compensation of underwriting staff
12. Required insurance
13. Types of borrower
14. Geographic dispersion
15. Please describe any internal rating system and its potential relation to public rating agency ratings.
16. Are the underwriting criteria revised and updated on a frequent basis? What are the factors that influence this and how often is this done?

(Please provide copies of loan applications and terms and conditions. How does this compare with the overall market? Please provide a copy of your underwriting guidelines.)

(continued)

EXHIBIT 6.6 (*continued*)

Interest Rates

1. Do rates vary among products?
2. Floating rate loans: What is the frequency of loan rate resetting? How is the rate determined? How much notice is given to borrowers? How are borrowers notified?
3. How competitive are your interest rates?

Payments

1. How often are loan payments due?
2. On what day(s) of the month are payments made?
3. How are payments made: cash, check, direct debit?

Prepayments

1. Are borrowers allowed to prepay?
2. Is the size of the prepayment limited?
3. What is your rate of prepayments per month/year?
4. Explain the reasons for prepayments.
5. Are penalties charged for prepayments? If so, what is the penalty? Can it be waived?

Servicing/Arrears

1. Explain the servicing system and collection process.
2. Is servicing centralized within your institution?
3. Is servicing done within your institution?
4. Do you have the systems capability to transfer servicing to an unaffiliated entity? If so, how long would this take and at what cost?
5. Do you have a separate servicing department for loans in arrears?
6. How large is your arrears staff and what is their experience?
7. What is the number of delinquent loans per servicing employee?
8. Explain the collection procedure for arrears. When/how often is a delinquent borrower contacted? How is he contacted? By telephone? By mail? Is all collection activity done in house? If not, when are outside collectors used?
9. Are arrears/defaults seasonal?
10. Describe the primary causes of arrears and defaults. Do they increase with loans with higher loan-to-value ratios? Do they increase with

EXHIBIT 6.6 (*continued*)

---

larger loans? Are they particular to specific loan products or type? Do they vary from year of origination or level of seasoning?
11. What legal costs are involved? Do you use an in-house counsel?
12. Arrears/default reporting: How are arrears defined? Discuss computer tracking of arrears.

Foreclosure Process

1. How long is a company delinquent before enforcement proceedings are begun?
2. What are the specific procedures for foreclosure?
3. What data/documentation is necessary to carry out a foreclosure? Where is it stored? Who is eligible to access it?
4. What is the average foreclosure period (from the first day of borrower default to distribution of sale proceeds)?
5. What are the costs of foreclosure (legal, dealer fees, etc.)?

Company Loan Performance

1. What are the historical and current arrears (over the last 3–5 years) for your company loan portfolio? Please break down the data by: 1 to 30 days, 31 to 60 days, 61 to 90 days, 90 to 180 days, and >180 days.
2. As a percentage, what are the historical defaults for the last 5 years (i.e., loans that are actually foreclosed on) on a gross and net basis?
3. Historically (last 5 years) and on average, what percent is lost on each defaulted loan?
4. Recovery levels and the timing of recoveries for the past 3 to 5 years.

Document Storage

1. Where are loan documents stored? On site or off site? Explain the security arrangements.
2. Is the vault fireproof?
3. Do you have extra copies of the documents?
4. Are the documents copied onto microfiche or scanned electronically?

Computer Systems/Software

1. Is software a purchased package or was it developed in house?
2. Do any computer backup facilities exist?

(*continued*)

EXHIBIT 6.6 (*continued*)

3. Is a daily backup procedure in place?
4. What are the procedures for a disaster recovery?
5. Can/will the system identify securitized loans?
6. Can the system break down the company loan portfolio by loan characteristic?
7. Can the system provide historical data on company loan performance with respect to delinquencies, defaults, and prepayments?

Future Perspective

1. How do you view the future company finance market?
2. Do you envisage increased volume? Explain how and why.
3. Do you foresee a shift in lenders' market shares?
4. Do you think more lenders will enter the market?
5. Do you anticipate changing your underwriting standards to suit market demands?

III. Legal

General Market

1. What laws and government/financial entities regulate company loan lending? Is there a maximum interest rate?
2. What kind of security does a lender have and how is this evidenced?
3. Upon bankruptcy how is this interest protected?
4. What documents are necessary to create a loan and between/among what parties are they created?
5. What remedies may a lender exercise upon a borrower default?
6. Discuss the protection of lien status and the possibility of intervening creditors (including tax authorities).
7. What protection does a lender have against borrower fraud?
8. What protection does a lender have against fraud by its employees? Is insurance available to cover such fraud?

Foreclosure Process

1. Does the lender always have the legal right to foreclose on a company loan? If so, must certain conditions exist? Can any party (creditors, mortgagors, tenants, etc.) prevent the lender from foreclosing on the loan?

EXHIBIT 6.6 *(continued)*

2. Are foreclosure proceedings regulated by law (i.e., the timing and steps involved)?
3. Explain the procedures and parties involved (a court, governmental body, etc.).
4. Aside from prior lien holders, who else has a right to the company sale proceeds (i.e., tax authorities, the courts, etc.)?
5. Is the lender entitled to full recovery of the loan obligation (outstanding principal, accrued interest, legal fees) or are its rights to foreclosure proceeds limited to an absolute amount or percentage? Conversely, is the lender entitled to any gains realized from the sale?
6. Is a borrower personally liable for any unsatisfied loan obligation if foreclosure proceeds are insufficient to fully pay off the obligation?

Transaction-Specific Concerns

1. May company loans be sold or assigned?
2. Must the sale or assignment be registered? If so, with whom? Explain the process.
3. What costs are incurred (transfer tax, registration, etc.)?
4. Must notice be given to borrowers if the loans are sold or assigned?
5. Must borrowers approve of the sale/assignment?
6. Who will hold the security documents?
7. Are there any rights that are not transferred? If so, what are they?
8. Upon bankruptcy, what sections of the legal code apply? What do they say with regard to borrower's obligations, creditor's rights, bankrupt entity's obligations?
9. Could any other party have any competing rights to the assets (including loans, investment securities, bank accounts) or payments from them?
10. What kind of security interest will the SPV have in the loans?
11. Describe the flow of funds starting with the borrower payments and ending with payments made to investors. Are payments made to any party (i.e., the servicer) ever commingled with its other funds? If so, for how long? What would happen to funds held with this party upon its bankruptcy or insolvency? Would the SPV have a valid and timely claim to these funds? What evidence would the SPV have to provide to prove its rights to these funds?

(continued)

EXHIBIT 6.6 (*continued*)

Overview of Data Required

The following is a summary of the data requirements for initial due diligence and the rating agency review. As we can see, it is quite granular and detailed.

Requirements for Preliminary Analysis We would require some basic pool stratification tables (e.g., loan size, yield, obligor concentrations, seasoning, delinquency buckets, etc.) for initiating analysis on possible structures.

Requirements for Rating Agency Process

Company Information

- Annual reports for the last three years
- Credit and collection policies
- Form of loan contract

Collateral Tape Information Requirement (on loan-by-loan basis)

- Loan number
- Obligor ID
- Obligor group
- Obligor domicile
- Term/revolving facility
- Current balance in drawn currency
- Drawn currency
- Current balance in EUR
- Coupon type or benchmark
- Margin over benchmark
- Current interest rate (= Benchmark + Margin or Fixed coupon)
- Internal rating
- Rating Fitch (or mapped)
- Rating S&P (or mapped)
- Rating Moody's (or mapped)
- Agent bank (where applicable)
- Collateral type
- Collateral value
- Moody's industry code
- Moody's industry

EXHIBIT 6.6 *(continued)*

- S&P industry code
- S&P industry
- Fitch industry code
- Fitch industry
- Issuing date
- Maturity date
- Interest/principal payment date
- Next coupon fixing date
- Principal payment frequency
- Interest payment frequency
- Bullet/amortizing

Historical Data

Rating agencies will require detailed historic information for each type of asset to be securitized. Following is an overview of the data required.

Origination

1.0 Total portfolio
1.1 Amortizing loans
1.2 Revolving loans
1.3 Syndicated loans
1.4 Bonds
1.5 Portfolio originated by the sponsor bank
1.6 Portfolio acquired from other banks

Delinquency (dynamic)

2.0 Total portfolio
2.1 Amortizing loans
2.2 Revolving loans
2.3 Syndicated loans
2.4 Bonds
2.5 Portfolio originated by the sponsor bank
2.6 Portfolio acquired from other banks

Defaults: Static Vintages by Quarter of Origination—Number of Accounts

3.1.0 Total portfolio
3.1.1 Amortizing loans

(continued)

EXHIBIT 6.6 (*continued*)

3.1.2 Revolving loans
3.1.3 Syndicated loans
3.1.4 Bonds
3.1.5 Portfolio originated by the sponsor bank
3.1.6 Portfolio acquired from other banks

Defaults: Static Vintages by Quarter of Origination—Amounts

3.2.0 Total portfolio
3.2.1 Amortizing loans
3.2.2 Revolving loans
3.2.3 Syndicated loans
3.2.4 Bonds
3.2.5 Portfolio originated by the sponsor bank
3.2.6 Portfolio acquired from other banks

Status since Default (NPL, rearranged, back to current): Static Vintages

4.0 Total portfolio: All loans defaulted regardless of the year of origination, by number of accounts

Recovery from NPL: Static Vintages

5.0 Total portfolio

Prepayment/Repayment

6.1 Amortizing loans
6.2 Revolving loans
6.3 Syndicated loans
6.4 Bonds

LOAN-LEVEL DATA: RATING AGENCY CHECKLIST

EXHIBIT 6.7 Rating agency checklist

Loan Information	Collateral information
Loan ID	Loan ID
Disbursement ID	Current balance
Obligor group ID	Collateral (Y/N)

EXHIBIT 6.7 (*continued*)

Loan Information	Collateral information
Branch code	Current collateral valuation date
Obligor ID	Coverage ration
Obligor category	Current mortgage valuation date
Obligor annual turnover (€)	Total current collateral amount
Obligor establishment year	Cash (€)
Bank client since (year)	Checks (€)
Bank internal rating	Debt securities (€)
Obligor region	Equities (€)
NACE Code 4	Mortgage—1st lien (€)
NACE Description 4	Mortgage—2nd lien (€)
Loan type	Mortgage—3rd lien (€)
Arranger (for bond loans)	Receivables (€)
Syndicated (Y/N)	Bank guarantee
Currency	Other physical collateral (€)
Total original balance	Personal guarantee (Y/N)
Total current balance	Corporate guarantee (Y/N)
Original balance underwritten by bank	Corporate guarantor
Current balance underwritten by bank	Guarantor bank internal rating
Issue date	Guarantor bank internal rating system
Maturity date	Guarantor Moody's external rating
Coupon type	Guarantor S&P external rating
Benchmark	Guarantor Fitch external rating
Margin over benchmark	
Current total interest rate	
Next coupon reset date	
Interest payment frequency (months)	
Repayment profile	
Principal payment frequency (months)	
Fixed installments amount	
First principal payment date	
Loan purpose	
Interest arrears amount	
Capital arrears amount	
Number of interest payments in arrears	
Number of capital payments in arrears	
Prepayment penalty (Y/N)	
Prepayment penalty (%)	

AGENDA FOR RATING AGENCY SITE VISIT

As we noted in Part Two, the final part of the rating agency review is the site visit, during which the originator presents details of its operations and the transaction in a formal meeting. The rating agency will also physically visit certain departments in the bank that are involved with the deal. Exhibit 6.8 is an example of a typical agenda for such a site visit meeting.

EXHIBIT 6.8 Typical agenda for rating agency site visit

Start	Item
15 min	Executive summary and transaction overview
30 min	Bank corporate overview
	Organization, reporting, audit function, etc.
15 min	Corporate loan market overview
60 min	Origination, underwriting, and servicing
	Bond loan product description
	Servicing
60 min	Credit risk management
40 min	Collections—NPL management
30 min	Computer systems
60 min	Site visit—Corporate Banking division

LEGAL COUNSEL REVIEW

As required during the initial due diligence of the balance sheet, Exhibit 6.9 is a list of the issues for review by the arranging bank's legal counsel.

EXHIBIT 6.9 Legal counsel review checklist

☐ Review each loan agreement to ascertain whether there are any restrictions in the loan agreement that may impact the ability of the bank to transfer its loan to Red Sea, or whether any consents are required from the borrower or any other party prior to the loan transfer.

☐ Review each loan agreement to ascertain whether there are restrictions in the loan agreement relating to securitization of the relevant loan.

EXHIBIT 6.9 (*continued*)

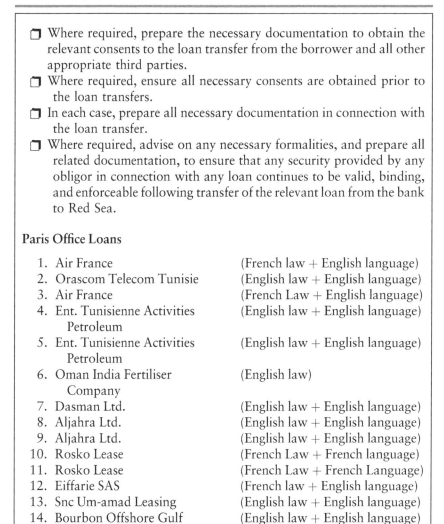

☐ Where required, prepare the necessary documentation to obtain the relevant consents to the loan transfer from the borrower and all other appropriate third parties.
☐ Where required, ensure all necessary consents are obtained prior to the loan transfers.
☐ In each case, prepare all necessary documentation in connection with the loan transfer.
☐ Where required, advise on any necessary formalities, and prepare all related documentation, to ensure that any security provided by any obligor in connection with any loan continues to be valid, binding, and enforceable following transfer of the relevant loan from the bank to Red Sea.

Paris Office Loans

1.	Air France	(French law + English language)
2.	Orascom Telecom Tunisie	(English law + English language)
3.	Air France	(French Law + English language)
4.	Ent. Tunisienne Activities Petroleum	(English law + English language)
5.	Ent. Tunisienne Activities Petroleum	(English law + English language)
6.	Oman India Fertiliser Company	(English law)
7.	Dasman Ltd.	(English law + English language)
8.	Aljahra Ltd.	(English law + English language)
9.	Aljahra Ltd.	(English law + English language)
10.	Rosko Lease	(French Law + French language)
11.	Rosko Lease	(French Law + French Language)
12.	Eiffarie SAS	(French law + English language)
13.	Snc Um-amad Leasing	(English law + English language)
14.	Bourbon Offshore Gulf	(English law + English language)
15.	Bourbon Offshore Gulf	(English law + English language)
16.	Lahwayla Leasing Ltd.	(English law + English language)
17.	Chateau Hotel Mont Royal	(French law + English language)
18.	Lahwayla Leasing Ltd.	(English law + English language)

French law total: 6
English law total: 12

(*continued*)

EXHIBIT 6.9 (*continued*)

Milan Office Loans

1. Oman India Fertiliser Company (English law)
2. Barilla Holding SpA (English law)
3. Barilla Holding SpA (English law)

Madrid Office Loans

1. Abengoa (Spanish law)
2. Befesa Zinc (Spanish law)
3. ACS Actividades de Construct . . . . (Spanish law)

Frankfurt Office Loans

1. Oiltanking Finance BV (German law)
2. STADA Arzneimittel AG (German law)

London Office Loans

1. AES Barka SAOC (English law)
2. El Behera Natural Gas Liqef Co SAE (English law)
3. [SembCorp Utilities (UK) Ltd. (English law)]
4. Idku Natural Gas Liquefaction Co. (English law)
5. ABC International re OBU Bahrain (English law)
6. Sidi Krir Generating Company (English law)
7. Sidi Krir Generating Company (English law)
8. Sidi Krir Generating Company (English law)
9. [SembCorp Utilities (UK) Limited (English law)]
10. [City Inn Ltd (English law)]
11. ENRC Marketing AG (English law)
12. AES Energia Cartagena (English law)
13. MezzVest Investments Ltd. (English law)
14. MezzVest Investments Ltd. (English law)
15. Spanish Egyptian Gas Company (English law)
16. Ajman Sewerage (Private) Co. Ltd. (English law)
17. Sabic Innovative Plastics B.V. (New York law)
18. Canyon Melezin SAS (English law with French law security)
19. [Sohar Aluminium Company (English law)]
20. Tata Steel Netherlands B.V. (English law)

EXHIBIT 6.9 *(continued)*

21.	[25 The North Colonnade Investment Co. Ltd.	(English law)]
22.	Autobahn Tank & Rast Holdings GmbH	(English law)
23.	Autobahn Tank & Rast Holdings GmbH	(English law)
24.	Autobahn Tank & Rast Holdings GmbH	(English law)
25.	Autobahn Tank & Rast Holdings GmbH	(English law)
26.	Brussels Airport Holding Co. SA	(English law)
27.	Brussels Airport Holding Co. SA	(English law)
28.	Trafigura Beheer BV Asia	(English law)
29.	Sovereign Hotels Ltd.	(English law; secured over property in UK)
30.	Hotel Les Airelles SAS	(French law + French language)
31.	Hotel Les Airelles SAS	(French law + French language)
32.	W2005/Thirty-Four B.V.	(English law)
33.	Kuwait Foreign Petroleum Exploration Co.	(English law)
34.	Dhofar Power Company SAOG	(English law)
35.	Dolphin Energy Ltd.	(English law; addition to list since 9/25/2009)

Total London loans at 10/30/2009 = 35
Total French law: 8
Total English law: 42
Total German law: 2
Total Spanish law: 3
Total New York law: 1
Total all branches loans = 57

FORM OF TRANSFER CERTIFICATE

A cash securitization requires the formal sale of the underlying assets to the SPV that forms the securitization deal. Exhibit 6.10 is an example of the template legal document used when transferring the loan from the bank balance sheet onto the SPV balance sheet. This example is an English law document.

EXHIBIT 6.10   Template for transfer certificate

SCHEDULE 1
FORM OF TRANSFER CERTIFICATE

To: [   ] as Agent and [   ] as Security Agent

From: *[The Existing Lender]* (the "**Existing Lender**") and *[The New Lender]* (the "**New Lender**")

Dated:

        [Parent] – [   ] Senior Facilities Agreement
        dated [   ] (the "**Facilities Agreement**")

1. We refer to the Facilities Agreement and to the Intercreditor Agreement (as defined in the Facilities Agreement). This agreement (the "**Agreement**") shall take effect as a Transfer Certificate for the purpose of the Facilities Agreement and as a Creditor/Agent Accession Undertaking for the purposes of the Intercreditor Agreement (and as defined in the Intercreditor Agreement). Terms defined in the Facilities Agreement have the same meaning in this Agreement unless given a different meaning in this Agreement.
2. We refer to clause [ ] (*Procedure for transfer*) of the Facilities Agreement:
   (a) The Existing Lender and the New Lender agree to the Existing Lender transferring to the New Lender by novation all or part of the Existing Lender's Commitment, rights and obligations referred to in the Schedule in accordance with Clause [ ] (*Procedure for transfer*).
   (b) The proposed Transfer Date is [ ].
   (c) The Facility Office and address, fax number, and attention details for notices of the New Lender for the purposes of Clause [ ] (*Addresses*) are set out in the Schedule.

EXHIBIT 6.10 (*continued*)

---

3. The New Lender expressly acknowledges the limitations on the Existing Lender's obligations set out in paragraph (c) of Clause [ ] (*Limitation of responsibility of Existing Lenders*).
4. The New Lender confirms, for the benefit of the Agent and without liability to any Obligor, that it is:
   (a) [a Qualifying Lender falling within paragraph (i)(A) [or paragraph (ii)] of the definition of Qualifying Lender);]
   (b) [a Treaty Lender;]
   (c) [not a Qualifying Lender].[1]
5. [The New Lender confirms that the person beneficially entitled to interest payable to that Lender in respect of an advance under a Finance Document is either:
   (a) a company resident in the United Kingdom for United Kingdom tax purposes;
   (b) a partnership each member of which is:
      (i) a company so resident in the United Kingdom; or
      (ii) a company not so resident in the United Kingdom which carries on a trade in the United Kingdom through a permanent establishment and which brings into account in computing its chargeable profits (within the meaning of section 19 of the CTA) the whole of any share of interest payable in respect of that advance that falls to it by reason of Part 17 of the CTA; or
   (c) a company not so resident in the United Kingdom which carries on a trade in the United Kingdom through a permanent establishment and which brings into account interest payable in respect of that advance in computing the chargeable profits (within the meaning of section 19 of the CTA) of that company.][2]

[5/6] The New Lender confirms that it [is]/[is not]* a Sponsor Affiliate.

(*continued*)

---

[1] Delete as applicable—each New Lender is required to confirm which of these three categories it falls within.
[2] Include if New Lender comes within paragraph (i)(B) of the definition of Qualifying Lender in Clause 18.1 (*Definitions*).
* Delete as applicable.

EXHIBIT 6.10   (*continued*)

[6/7]   [The New Lender confirms that it [is]/[is not]** a Non-Acceptable L/C Lender.]***

[7/8]   We refer to clause [18.5] (*Change of Senior Lender or Mezzanine Lender*) of the Intercreditor Agreement.

In consideration of the New Lender being accepted as a Senior Lender for the purposes of the Intercreditor Agreement (and as defined therein), the New Lender confirms that, as from the Transfer Date, it intends to be party to the Intercreditor Agreement as a Senior Lender, and undertakes to perform all the obligations expressed in the Intercreditor Agreement to be assumed by a Senior Lender and agrees that it shall be bound by all the provisions of the Intercreditor Agreement, as if it had been an original party to the Intercreditor Agreement.

[6/7]   This Agreement may be executed in any number of counterparts and this has the same effect as if the signatures on the counterparts were on a single copy of this Agreement.

[8/9]   This Agreement [and any non-contractual obligations arising out of or in connection with it] [is/are][3] governed by English law.

[9/10]   This Agreement has been entered into on the date stated at the beginning of this Agreement.

Note: The execution of this Transfer Certificate may not transfer a proportionate share of the Existing Lender's interest in the Transaction Security in all jurisdictions. It is the responsibility of the New Lender to ascertain whether any other documents or other formalities are required to perfect a transfer of such a share in the Existing Lender's Transaction Security in any jurisdiction and, if so, to arrange for execution of those documents and completion of those formalities.

** Delete as applicable.

*** Include only if the transfer includes the transfer of a Revolving Facility Commitment/a participation in the Revolving Facility.

[3] This clause should follow the approach adopted as regards non-contractual obligations in Clause [ ] (*Governing Law*). This should be done (and this footnote deleted) before the Agreement is signed.

EXHIBIT 6.10 *(continued)*

THE SCHEDULE

Commitment/rights and obligations to be transferred
[*insert relevant details*]
[*Facility Office address, fax number, and attention details for
notices and account details for payments*]

[Existing Lender]   [New Lender]
By: By:

This Agreement is accepted as a Transfer Certificate for the purposes
of the Facilities Agreement by the Agent, and as a Creditor/Agent Accession Undertaking for the purposes of the Intercreditor Agreement by the
Security Agent, and the Transfer Date is confirmed as [   ].

[Agent]
By:

[Security Agent]
By:

INVESTOR AND RATING AGENCY PRESENTATION TEMPLATE

During the site visit the originator will present to the rating agency, usually in
Microsoft PowerPoint format, all the aspects of the deal. Exhibit 6.11 is a
checklist of the content required for inclusion in the presentation. It is
exhaustive, but not rigid: The originator may choose to modify the content
to suit the specific nature of the transaction in question.

EXHIBIT 6.11 Investor and rating agency presentation checklist

Deal Summary
- Deal introduction
- Deal timing (road show dates, expected pricing)
- Capital structure
- Collateral features

Company Overview
- Background
- Ownership structure
- Management team
- Strategy
- Forecasts

[Country] Economy and [Asset Class] Market
- Macro environment
- Credit risk environment
- Competitors/Pricing evolution
- Forecast

Company [Asset Class] Business
- Core competencies
- Strategies to achieve goals
- Product mix
- Origination channels
- Marketing
- Underwriting process
- Credit scoring
- Collections/Servicing
- Foreclosure process

Portfolio Historic Performance

Transaction Structure and Terms
- Liability structure
- Transaction features
- Priority of payments
- Credit enhancement (over time)
- Indicative terms

Appendix
- Portfolio stratification tables
- Eligibility criteria

IN-HOUSE CREDIT RATING MAPPING CHART: LOWER AND UPPER VALUES

The bank will rate its transactions under an internal credit rating methodology. These also map to an equivalent external rating agency rating. Exhibit 6.12 shows the default probability values for an internal model and how these translate into an equivalent Moody's credit rating.

EXHIBIT 6.12   In-house credit rating mapping chart

MRA Grade		Default Probability (BPs)		Moody's	Bank
Lower Value	Upper Value	Lower Value	Upper Value		
0	0	0.01	0.06	Aaa	1
0	0	0.06	0.14	Aa1	2
0	0	0.14	0.29	Aa2	2
0	0	0.3	0.59	Aa3	2
0	0.86	0.6	1.09	A1	3
0.87	1.55	1.1	3.9	A2	3
1.56	2.04	4	8.9	A3	3
2.05	2.42	9	16.9	Baa1	4
2.43	2.78	17	41.9	Baa2	4
2.79	3.96	42	86.9	Baa3	4
3.97	5.47	87	155.9	Ba1	5
5.48	6.35	156	303.9	Ba2	5
6.36	6.89	304	467.9	Ba3	5
6.90	8.06	468	715.9	B1	6
8.07	9.04	716	1,161.9	B2	6
9.05	9.38	1,162	1,737.9	B3	6
9.39	9.86	1,738	2,599.9	Caa1	7
9.87	9.99	2,600	5,098.9	Caa2	7
10.00	10.00	5,099	-	Caa3	7

RATING AGENCY PRESENTATION: CORPORATE BANK ORIGINATION PROCESSES

Exhibit 6.13 is a pro forma template of the baseline content of a rating agency presentation. This is the business line section of the presentation, showing the processes used by the corporate banking department when originating new loans.

EXHIBIT 6.13 Template of the baseline content of a rating agency presentation

---

BRIDGE TO MENA

The bank has a defined Bridge to MENA strategy, developing business from our European branch network to the MENA region. We work with our parent branch network in the MENA region, as well as correspondent banking partners to provide a wide footprint.

Network	MENA Network	
Austria	Abu Dhabi	Oman
France	Algeria	Palestine
Germany	Bahrain	Saudi Arabia
Italy	Dubai	Syria
Spain	Egypt	Tunisia
United Kingdom	Jordan	UAE
	Lebanon	Yemen Republic
	Morocco	

CORPORATE BANK DIVISION STRUCTURE

- CIB has industry specialists with pan-European coverage, assisted by product specialists where required, and supported by a network of Arab bank branches and correspondent banks managed by the Financial Institutions group.
- Each team is led by an industry/product head, who has responsibility for coverage across our European branch network. Each head will have between two and five relationship directors covering their industry across the six geographies where EAB is present. Each RD may cover up to two industries.
- Credit is an independent part of the bank, but an essential part of the origination process.

EXHIBIT 6.13 Divisional Structure (*continued*)

MD CIB

Construction and Infrastructure | Energy, Power, and Natural Resources | Manufacturing and Engineering | Real Estate and Hotels | Transport and Logistics | Commodities and Trade Finance — Industries

Trade Finance | Project Finance | Islamic Finance — Products

Financial Institutions Group — Network

EXHIBIT 6.13   *(continued)*

ORIGINATION PROCESS

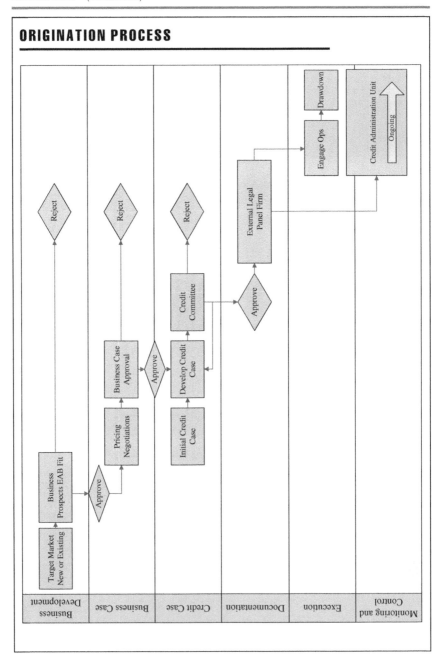

EXHIBIT 6.13 (*continued*)

- **Business Development.** EAB has a very clearly defined strategy of building a Bridge to MENA and we are putting this strategy into action through focusing on a defined target market. EAB's value proposition is our access to the group network throughout the MENA region and the target market will comprise those companies with a European and MENA footprint. Target market customers will be relationship based rather than transaction based, and filtered according to their fit with EAB's industry and geographic coverage, while meeting our risk and return hurdles. The RDs are responsible for growing their client base, having already defined existing and prospective clients based on the filters above.
- **Business Case.** Once a prospective deal is in progress, the RD will submit a business case request. This approval is based on the effective use of capital and limits, while working within defined country and industry limits. The business case is approved by the MD CIB and the portfolio manager.
- **Credit Case.** The RD, with assistance from a credit risk analyst or associate relationship director, will have completed an initial credit review prior to submitting the business case. Once the business case is approved, the detailed credit review will be completed and submitted to the Credit Committee. Depending on the size of the deal, the deal can be approved by the head of credit (independent to CIB), EAB Credit Committee, EAB Board Panel, or submitted to the head office in Jordan. The deal may be approved or rejected outright, or may be returned subject to further analysis.
- **Documentation.** External legal counsel is normally engaged for documentation. EAB has a mix of bilateral and syndicated deals, and always engages our own counsel. EAB has panel-approved law firms, which includes magic circle, as well as second-tier firms.
- **Execution.** As the documentation process reaches its conclusion, Operations will be engaged to ensure the loan booking and funding are set up correctly. The Credit Administration Unit will also have been engaged to input the limits and set up a monitoring process for the deal, which will include loan covenants and measurement and diarizing financial information requirements.
- **Ongoing Monitoring.** The Credit Administration Unit collects and tests covenants as defined in the documentation. The RD also completes a credit review on an annual basis, which will be submitted to the same credit committee that it was approved by.

(*continued*)

EXHIBIT 6.13 (*continued*)

PRODUCTS AND PRICING

- CIB has a return on capital hurdle when considering new business. The hurdle is assessed on a relationship basis, so individual products may not meet the hurdle on a stand-alone basis, but additional factors such as current accounts, treasury sales, and trade volumes may add to the overall relationship value.
- There are three main credit-based products: vanilla Treasury products along with operating accounts.
- Current prices are now around twice that available pre-crunch.
- The majority of the book is around BBB, with the next-largest exposure in the AAA/AA region, due to ECA-backed deals, structured transactions, or high-quality counterparties.

Product	Product Risk Weighting	AAA/AA	A	BBB	BB
Loans	100%	40bps	100bps	200bps	250bps+
Guarantees	50%	20bps	40bps	75bps	125bps
Letters of Credit	20%	LC income is primarily small-ticket values, which incur minimum charges, so are not margin driven. There may be discounting on the back of LCs.			
Swaps	Dependent on Term/CCY, etc.	Sufficient to achieve ROC hurdle, in conjunction with other offerings.			
Current Accounts	Nil	Transaction charges plus value of CR interest spread (dependent on interest rates).			

LOAN TRANSFER SCHEDULE OF TASKS

Exhibit 6.14 shows the actual loan transfer schedule used in the Red Sea ABS transaction. This shows the internal process used, line by line, to transfer the underlying assets from the originating bank to the Red Sea SPV. This process involves the IT and back office operations (settlement) departments, as well as the front office and legal departments.

EXHIBIT 6.14   Red Sea ABS loan transfer schedule

Red Sea Securitization - Schedule of Tasks and Responsibilities	Start Date	End Date	Responsibility
Project Governance	8/25/2009 8:00	9/14/2009 14:00	
Meeting to discuss scope and test approach	8/25/2009 8:00	8/25/2009 9:00	All
Document test approach and review	8/25/2009 9:00	9/2/2009 9:00	
Provide test case template to Treasury	8/25/2009 9:00	8/25/2009 14:00	
Agree test dates and test resources with business units	8/25/2009 9:00	8/26/2009 9:00	
Set up daily test status meetings	9/14/2009 9:00	9/14/2009 14:00	
Prepare test issue log	9/2/2009 9:00	9/2/2009 14:00	
Prepare Test Environments	9/2/2009 8:00	9/10/2009 12:00	
Equation (test partition)	9/2/2009 8:00	9/8/2009 17:00	
System restore from production (correct system date)	9/2/2009 8:00	9/3/2009 17:00	
Set up new entities	9/4/2009 8:00	9/7/2009 17:00	
Red Sea Master Series Purchase Trust Limited	9/4/2009 8:00	9/7/2009 17:00	
Red Sea Master Series Limited	9/4/2009 8:00	9/7/2009 17:00	
Static data configuration	9/8/2009 8:00	9/8/2009 17:00	
Findur Test Database	9/7/2009 8:00	9/7/2009 12:00	
Take a copy of production database (on correct system date)	9/7/2009 8:00	9/7/2009 12:00	
Interfaces	9/7/2009 13:00	9/10/2009 12:00	

(continued)

EXHIBIT 6.14 *(continued)*

Red Sea Securitization - Schedule of Tasks and Responsibilities	Start Date	End Date	Responsibility
Suffix Hunter (Findur/Equation) interface up and running	9/7/2009 13:00	9/7/2009 15:00	
Findur/Swift interface (Trace Module running on SR2009 upgrade version)	9/7/2009 13:00	9/9/2009 12:00	
Connectivity test successful	9/9/2009 13:00	9/10/2009 12:00	
User Access	9/9/2009 8:00	9/9/2009 12:00	
Ensure all test resources have access to the test environments and provide password details	9/9/2009 8:00	9/9/2009 12:00	
Prepare Test Cases/Test Scenarios	8/25/2009 14:00	9/15/2009 17:00	
Treasury	8/27/2009 8:00	9/10/2009 17:00	
Operations	8/25/2009 14:00	9/9/2009 14:00	
Finance	8/25/2009 14:00	9/9/2009 14:00	
Middle office	8/25/2009 14:00	9/9/2009 14:00	
Valuation control	8/25/2009 14:00	9/9/2009 14:00	
Credit	8/25/2009 14:00	9/9/2009 14:00	
Document test transactions/scenarios	9/11/2009 8:00	9/14/2009 17:00	
Review and sign-off before user acceptance testing (UAT) commences	9/15/2009 8:00	9/15/2009 17:00	
Test entry criteria complete	9/15/2009 17:00	9/15/2009 17:00	

EXHIBIT 6.14 *(continued)*

Red Sea Securitization - Schedule of Tasks and Responsibilities	Start Date	End Date	Responsibility
Test Phase (UAT)	9/16/2009 8:00	10/7/2009 17:00	
Test Cycle 1	9/16/2009 8:00	9/22/2009 14:00	
Loans booked in EAB Equation cancelled and rebooked in the name of Red Sea Master Series Purchase Trust Limited	9/16/2009 8:00	9/16/2009 10:00	
London funding deals that are currently booked in Open Link with business line amended to be booked with the ALCO portfolio	9/16/2009 10:00	9/16/2009 12:00	
Branch funding deals cancelled in Open Link and re-input between Treasury and the ALCO portfolio	9/16/2009 13:00	9/16/2009 15:00	
Pass-through certificate between the two Red Sea entities booked in Equation	9/16/2009 15:00	9/16/2009 17:00	
Issuance of the securities by Red Sea Master Series Limited booked in Equation	9/17/2009 8:00	9/17/2009 10:00	
EAB's purchase of the securitized assets booked in Open Link in the ALCO portfolio	9/17/2009 10:00	9/17/2009 12:00	
Run Suffix Hunter	9/17/2009 13:00	9/17/2009 15:00	
Run EOD in Findur; check output	9/17/2009 15:00	9/17/2009 16:00	
Check postings in Equation	9/17/2009 16:00	9/18/2009 11:00	

(continued)

EXHIBIT 6.14 *(continued)*

Red Sea Securitization - Schedule of Tasks and Responsibilities	Start Date	End Date	Responsibility
Run COA (Chart of accounts) in Equation	9/18/2009 11:00	9/18/2009 14:00	
Run Equation EOD	9/18/2009 14:00	9/21/2009 14:00	
Check EOD reports	9/21/2009 14:00	9/22/2009 14:00	
Report test issues to testing coordinator	9/22/2009 14:00	9/23/2009 9:00	
Test Cycle 2	9/22/2009 14:00	9/24/2009 14:00	
Regression/Retest of test cycle 1	9/22/2009 14:00	9/24/2009 14:00	
Document test results and test evidence	9/22/2009 14:00	9/23/2009 14:00	
Test ongoing processes (repayment, etc.)	9/22/2009 14:00	9/23/2009 14:00	
Testing Sign-Off for Go-Live	9/23/2009 14:00	9/24/2009 14:00	
All BUs provide UAT sign-off/test evidence/completed test cases to test coordinator	9/23/2009 14:00	9/24/2009 14:00	
Implementation tasks	10/1/2009 8:00	10/7/2009 17:00	
Go-Live	10/7/2009 17:00	10/7/2009 17:00	

LOAN TRANSFERS, ACCOUNTING MOVEMENTS

Exhibit 6.15 is a summary of the accounting treatment of the liabilities issued as part of the Red Sea deal, and the process under which the originator purchased the issued notes. This was an in-house deal, but the treatment for accounting purposes would be no different for an external purchaser.

EXHIBIT 6.15 Red Sea Loan transfers, accounting movements summary

Liabilities		Assets	

EAB LDN CIB FUND

<no liability>	0		
	0		0

EAB LDN MM

Market Counterparty	12,288,749		
		Internal asset - EAB LDN ALCO	12,288,749
	12,288,749		12,288,749

EAB LDN ALCO (securitization)

		Purchase ABS security - issuer = RED SEA M SERIES	12,300,000
			0
Internal liability - EAB LDN MM	12,288,749		
	12,288,749		12,300,000

RED SEA PUR TRUST

<Internal liability - pass-through note - RED SEA M SERIES>	12,288,749	Loan - ORASCOM	828,749
Cash Reserve (BNP account)	11,251	Loan - MEZZVEST	11,460,000
	12,300,000		12,288,749

(continued)

EXHIBIT 6.15 *(continued)*

Liabilities		Assets	
		RED SEA M SERIES	
Sell ABS security - ctpy = EAB ALCO	12,300,000	*<Internal asset - pass-through note - RED SEA PUR TRUST>*	12,288,749
		<risk balance>	11,251
	12,300,000		12,300,000

SIGN-OFF DOCUMENT: SECURITIZATION PROJECT

As part of the internal risk management of the transaction, all relevant department heads are required to sign off their approval of the correctness of the process. Exhibit 6.16 is an example of such a sign-off document.

EXHIBIT 6.16 Red Sea securitization project internal sign-off document

I confirm that as Department/Function Head of _____ that:

1. The impact of the securitization on existing risks, audit points, and other issues of which departmental management is aware has been assessed and is not expected to contravene the EAB risk appetite or policies.
   Refer to the EAB Risk Map.
2. That all and any new risks (including any appropriate action plans) created as a result of the implementation of the securitization have been documented, assessed, and mitigated in an issues/risk log and do not contravene the EAB risk appetite.

EXHIBIT 6.16 (*continued*)

Refer to the EAB Risk Appetite Statement and EAB Risk Appetite Measures documents.

3. That the impact of the securitization on any internal or regulatory limits/conditions/guidelines has been assessed and is not expected to result in any breaches.
4. That there are no outstanding tasks to be completed before the securitization go-live and the department is ready to operationally support the securitization.
5. That the departmental policy and control/procedures documentation has been reviewed and updated.
6. That all relevant staff have received any training necessary to support the securitization.
7. That the departmental business continuity plan has been updated and any contingency measures tested.
8. That any data submitted to third parties is accurate and has been verified.

Signed: _____

Name (block letters): _____

Date: _____

PLEASE FORWARD SIGNED DOCUMENT TO OPERATIONAL RISK CONTROL

SECURITIZATION TESTING: FINANCE DEPARTMENT

For a first-time issuer, we recommend that prior to the actual transfer and closing the bank tests the transfer and booking process, and associated accounting movements, of the transaction. Exhibit 6.17 is a rundown of the testing that took place in this regard for the Red Sea project.

EXHIBIT 6.17 Red Sea securitization testing—Finance department

1. Testing Undertaken

Following input of deals by Operations (Equations) and Treasury (OpenLink), and IT running End of Day (EOD), Finance tested the following:

(a) Calculation of interest posted to the profit and loss (P&L) on the maturing of loans in EAB

(b) Accounting entries generated from all steps of the transaction process

(c) Chart of accounts to ensure all postings to the general ledger (GL) balanced

2. Testing Results

(a) Calculation of interest posted to the P&L on the maturing of loans in EAB

The following table shows the amount of interest expected to have accrued on each loan vs the automatic P&L posting on the forced maturity of the loan:

EXHIBIT 6.17 (*continued*)

Deal Reference	Branch	Customer	Customer Full Name Gfcun	CCY	Current Deal Amount	Interest Rate Actual Rate	Last Interest Cycle Date	Interest Days Basis	Expected Interest Posting	Actual Interest Posting
CL11010117002	PARI	412155	CHATEAU HOTEL MONT ROYAL SAS	EUR	14,000,000.00	2.757	14-Jul-09	ACT/360	93,278.50	93,278.50
CL0000835001	CITY	411353	AES ENERGIA CARTAGENA	EUR	39,064,817.47	1.339	30-Sep-09	ACT/360	13,076.95	13,076.95
CL11010040001	PARI	26587	DASMAN LTD	USD	3,204,609.55	5.99	13-Jul-09	ACT/360	46,922.61	46,922.61
CL0000852001	CITY	411507	AJMAN SEWERAGE (PRIVATE) LTD COMPANY	USD	50,000,000.00	1.05438	09-Sep-09	ACT/360	43,932.50	42,601.21

EXHIBIT 6.17   *(continued)*

All but one of the loans posted the exact figure anticipated.

Issue 1: Deal CL00000852001 posted $1,331.29 less than expected.
   (b) Accounting entries generated from all steps of the transaction
   process
   (i) Loans matured in EAB & rebooked in name of SPV
        Operations matured the loans in Equations, amend-
        ing the SSIs so no nostros/current accounts would be
        affected. The entries expected on the maturing of the
        loan for the nominal were:
           Cr. Customer Loan Account
           Dr. Red Sea Funding
        The preceding happened accordingly.
Issue 2: On the maturing of the deal, interest accrued credited the
P&L and debited the Red Sea Funding account. As Red Sea
Funding only took on the nominal, the EAB counterparty
account in RSPT is not equal to the Red Sea counterparty in
EAB. See the following example: This is because the original
loans were matured in EAB as principal + accrued but the
loans as bought by RSPT and the pass-through notes were
done at principal only. The RSPT and RSMS notes are issued
at par but with notional that is equal to the market value (dirty
price) of loans sold from EAB.

Deal Reference	Branch	Basic	Account Short Name	Account Type	Currency	Posting CCY
LBGCL00000835001	CITY	964143	I/R S/LN PRSCOS	IE	EUR	13,076.95
LBGCL00000835001	CITY	638641	RED SEA FUNDING	CA	EUR	−39,077,894.42
LBGCL00000835001	CITY	411353	CARTAGENA TA	BG	EUR	39,064,817.47
LBGCL00000000002	RSPT	411353	AES ENERGIA	BG	EUR	−39,064,817.47
LBGCL00000000002	RSPT	639419	EAB SECURITIZE	CA	EUR	39,064,817.47

EXHIBIT 6.17 *(continued)*

(ii) Pass-through certificate
Operations booked the pass-through certificates using new deal types. As expected, the following transactions happened:
In RSPT:
Dr. Red Sea Master Series Current Account
Cr. Red Sea Master Series Pass-Through Liability Account
In RSMS:
Dr. Red Sea Funding Pass-Through Asset Account
Cr. Red Sea Funding Current Account
Issue 3: There was no posting for day 1 accrued interest on either the notes issued or purchased; as expected these are 0 accrued interest on day 1.
(iii) FRN sold and purchased
In Equations, Operations booked the FRNs (2 EUR & 2 USD) using the new deal type FNS. As expected, the following transactions happened:
In RSMS:
Dr. EAB Securitization Current Account
Cr. EAB Securitization FRN Liability
Issue 4: There was no posting for day 1 accrued interest as before.
In OpenLink, Treasury booked the FRNs purchased by EAB. This generated the following entries:
In EAB:
Dr. Red Sea Master Series FRN asset for notional
Cr. Clearstream for notional
Dr. Red Sea Master Series FRN Interest Receivable for interest
Cr. Bonds Interest (P&L)
In terms of the accounting, these all seem fine.
Issue 5: I cannot tie up the interest posting with the deal details.
(c) Chart of Accounts to ensure all postings to the GL balanced
After EODs had been run, COA reports were run from Hyperion to check the integrity of the balance sheet.
Issue 6: After accounts had all been classified, balance sheet for City and Cannes did not balance. RSPT & RSPS both balanced. Many users could be posting various entries to Singapore Test, this may be the cause of the imbalances, as the transactions posted have all balanced.

ACCOUNTING PROCESS ON CLOSING

On closing the deal, the originator will account for the movements on its balance sheet. Exhibit 6.18 is a summary of this process.

EXHIBIT 6.18 Closing process summary

Step 1: Loans Are Matured in EAB and Rebooked in RSPT

When the loans are matured, a credit will be posted on the customer loan account and the debit will usually go to either a nostro or customer current account. Ops will have to amend the SSI so the debit will go to:

1001-638641-301 (USD) RED SEA FUNDING CA
1001-638641-345 (EUR) RED SEA FUNDING CA

When the loans are rebooked, there will be a debit on the customer loan account. The credit entry that would usually go over nostro/current account will instead pass over:

1009-639419-301 (USD) EAB SECURITIZATION CA
1009-639419-345 (EUR) EAB SECURITIZATION CA

Step 2: Pass-Through Certificate Is Booked in RSPT & RSMS

Ops will book the two deal tickets provided by Treasury. New deal types have been created to give an accurate reflection of this transaction. These deal types are a copy of SDS & SLS, with the only differences being the three-letter abbreviation, the name of the deal type, and the nominal account type attached (new account types have been created for this purpose).

In RSPT, the liability issued will be booked as deal type **PTS** and will credit:

1009-638668 RED SEA MASTER SERIES LTD. Suffixes for USD & EUR will auto-open on account type **PT**, a new account type with the same characteristics as a DA (fixed-term deposit)

EXHIBIT 6.18 *(continued)*

In RSMS, the asset purchased will be booked as deal type **PTP** and will debit:

1008-638641 RED SEA FUNDING. Suffixes for USD & EUR will auto-open on account type **PV**, a new account type with the same characteristics as an AA (fixed-term loan)

Step 3: FRN Issued by RSMS, Purchased by EAB

Ops will book the four deal tickets provided by Treasury. A new deal type has been created to give an accurate reflection of this transaction. The deal type is a copy of SDS, with the only differences being the three-letter abbreviation, the name of the deal type, and the nominal account type attached (a new account type has been created for this purpose).

In RSMS, the liabilities issued will be booked as deal type **FNS**, and will credit:

1009-639419 EAB SECURITIZATION. Suffixes for USD & EUR will auto-open on account type **PU**, a new account type with the same characteristics as a DA (fixed-term deposit)

The FRN purchased by EAB will be booked in OpenLink by Treasury, and I imagine this will be debiting:

1001-638668 –LY

The result from these steps will be that on a consolidated basis, 639419, 638641, and 638668 will net to zero.

EUR JUNIOR TRANCHE TRADE TICKET

Exhibit 6.19 is the trade ticket used to book each underlying loan asset when selling from the originator to the Red Sea SPV. The example shown is for the EUR-denominated junior tranche, and has been booked into the Asset and Liability Committee (ALCO) book of the originating bank. This is because the transaction was an in-house deal. If this was a conventional third-party deal, the ticket would have the same content but be booked to the external purchaser.

EXHIBIT 6.19   Red Sea Master Series Ltd trade with EAB ALCO (junior tranche)

Input by Treasury		Part A
ABS - J Number: [ ]	Trade Date	10.13.09
Lend / Borrow	**Amount**	**CCY**
Borrow	5,406,482	EUR
Start Date	**Interest Rate**	
10.15.09	6 month Euribor + 70 bps	
Maturity Date	**Counterparty**	
12.30.27	EAB ALCO	
Accounting Group	**Accounting Area**	
LONDON		
Sales ID		
Insert sales ID		

An ALCO book is one held centrally at a bank; that is, not attributed to any one business line.

SENIOR TRANCHE TRADE TICKET

We show the senior tranche trade ticket in Exhibit 6.20.

EXHIBIT 6.20   Red Sea Master Series Ltd trade with EAB ALCO (senior tranche)

Input by Treasury		Part A
ABS - S Number: [ ]	Trade Date	10.13.09
Lend / Borrow	**Amount**	**CCY**
Borrow	48,658,336	EUR
Start Date	**Interest Rate**	
10.15.09	6 month Euribor + 40 bps	
Maturity Date	**Counterparty**	
12.30.27	EAB ALCO	
Accounting Group	**Accounting Area**	
LONDON		
Sales ID		
Insert sales ID		

INTERNAL TRANSFER BOOKING PROCESS

EXHIBIT 6.21   Internal transfer booking process used during the Red Sea closing

- The issuance of the Red Sea Bonds will be booked within Equation for the Red Sea Master Series issuing vehicle. The bonds will be booked as a floating-rate loan, as and when it is necessary to adjust the nominal amount of the loans (as an underlying loan is repaid) a close and rebooking of the bonds will happen in Equation.
- The purchase of the bonds for the ALCO book will be booked in OpenLink in the same manner as any other FRN that is currently purchased from an external counterparty, again as an adjustment is needed to be made to the nominal value of the bonds a one-step amend will be booked to match the new booking in Equation.
- Operations will send out a draft template to be filled in by the relevant departments (Treasury, Ops, Finance, IT) that will log what we expect to see as a result of the test bookings.
- The test process will cover
  - Sale of loans from EAB to Red Sea Purchase Trust (Equation) and purchase of loans by Red Sea from EAB (Equation)
  - Amendment of funding ticket by Treasury from Corporate Banking to ALCO (OpenLink)
  - The issuance of the pass-through note from Red Sea Purchase Trust to Red Sea Master Series (Equation)
  - The issuance of notes by Red Sea Master Series (Equation)
  - Purchase of notes by EAB (ALCO book) from Red Sea Master Series (Open Link)
- Operations will attempt the test transfer in third week of September.

QUESTIONS FROM TRUSTEE, PAYING AGENT, AND SERVICES PROVIDER

Typically, all securitization deals will appoint a third-party trustee for the issuer SPV, and the issued notes may also require a paying agent. The SPV itself will also generally have a third-party administrator appointed. Exhibit 6.22 is a checklist of the issues that the service provider will ask as part of its review work after being appointed, but ahead of the closing date. These points need to be considered by the originator as part of the closing process.

EXHIBIT 6.22 Service provider checklist

Agent Banks and Information Flow

- EAB Ops had initially thought it best to receive loan info from agents and bounce to BNP thereafter.
- Given that the agents are advised via the transfer certificate of the handover to Red Sea and all the required payment details post closure, there is consideration for BNP to receive all loan information in the first instance and then bounce to EAB.
- Who is responsible for issuing the transfer certificate to the agent banks? When will this process be started/drafted (the timelines required to assume all sign-offs from agents agree to the transfer could potentially take some time)? Are there any communications that EAB Operations are expected to undertake? A fee is required to be paid for each transfer. Is this assumed to be paid by EAB?
- How many different agent banks are on the existing loan cut? How many different institutions is EAB engaging with regarding transfer certificate sign-off?
- When is Red Sea likely to be confirmed as established and how is this communicated to BNP? Once the company is officially registered, then Red Sea is able to have accounts set up at BNP (and we can obtain details for our records and systems).

Closure and Settlement

- General consensus is that a free-of-payment, netted settlement would suit both parties best. This process would include the payment of residual/balance funds only with the securities and loan sales netted accordingly.
- EAB Ops (for good record and monitor) should devise a closure checklist and spreadsheet to ensure each of the loans is signed for transfer by the agent and that they are transferred accordingly.
- Regarding payments to EAB from Red Sea: What are the Ops responsibilities to ensure this gets done, who contacts BNP to move monies at closure and so forth, and what are our closure responsibilities regarding the loans? What are our closure responsibilities regarding the securities?
- What is the order of closure events and what are our overall R&Rs (linked to the above two points)?

EXHIBIT 6.22 (*continued*)

- EAB's accruals at point of closure need to be known in order that correct interest apportionment is afforded to EAB/Red Sea. How is this assumed to work? Are we selling the loans at a price that includes accrued to date? Or are we expecting to receive a portion of interest at the end of the existing loan periods?
- Who applies for/sets up the ISIN for the securities? EAB or BNP?

Ongoing Management and Processing of the Structure

- At closure the loan value vs. note value should be pretty much equal.
- As time passes and the loans are slowly amortized, the loan value + cash account balance should be pretty much equal the note value.
- How much residual cash do we want to carry in the account before we either repay a portion of the note or else purchase more loans to top-up the portfolio?
- How many accounts are envisaged to be in the overall structure (i.e., reserve account, collection account, fee account)?
- Has EAB established all the apportionment of fees, interest, and so on with BNP? Has this been agreed on?
- Can BNP management fees be taken from the SPV if EAB pays the required amounts into the account prior to fee due date?
- MT950 requirement and ledger file feed to Intellimatch for account and nostro reconciliation on behalf of Red Sea: Is this required? If so, Control needs to be engaged to ensure the ledger file includes all the necessary information and the external Red Sea Account with BNP is notified in order that a separate balance pool can be established in Intellimatch. Do we want to have our own reconciliation? Frequency: daily, weekly, monthly?
- Operations will likely need to be signatories for Red Sea in order to ensure smooth and efficient running of the operation.
- Bank report required to monitor the level of drawings for Red Sea Loans that are yet to be fully committed.
- Red Sea internal e-mail group to be established to include all relevant stakeholders. Post go live, the recipients can be amended to business as usual (BAU) staff only.

SUMMARY AND CONCLUSIONS

This chapter will have highlighted just what an involved project management process a securitization transaction is. Much of the activity in an ABS deal takes place in parallel, and it is one of the few product types that involves virtually every department of the originating bank in the closing process. The templates and checklists exhibited in this chapter are all live actual worksheets and applicable in most securitization cases. We hope they prove to be of value, particularly to first-time originators.

About the Authors

Suleman Baig has worked for Deutsche Bank AG for more than 10 years and is currently with their credit structuring team. He has extensive experience dealing with first-time issuers and has structured a number of market-first securitization transactions (both agency and principal) in a variety of asset classes and jurisdictions. These include the first auto ABS to come from Ireland, the first Greek RMBS from an unrated bank, and the first synthetic UK PFI CLO to include NHS LIFT assets. Suleman has also worked in Covered Bond transactions, and structured the first Covered Bond Programmes to come from Portugal, Greece, Belgium, and Finland. He structured the first Covered Bond to be issued from Latin America, originated by Global Bank in Panama and awarded "Structured Trade of the Year" for 2012 by *Latin Finance.*

Suleman graduated in Mathematics from the London School of Economics.

Moorad Choudhry is Treasurer, Corporate Banking Division at the Royal Bank of Scotland. He was previously head of treasury at Europe Arab Bank, head of treasury at KBC Financial Products, and vice president in structured finance services at JPMorgan Chase Bank. While at KBC FP he led the structuring team that closed Picaros Funding, the world's first multi-SPV synthetic ABCP conduit and winner of *Euromoney*'s "Structured Finance Deal of the Year" award for 2005.

Moorad is visiting professor at the Department of Mathematical Sciences, Brunel University, visiting teaching fellow at the Department of Management, Birkbeck, University of London, and vice-chair of the Board of Directors of PRMIA. He is on the editorial board of the *Journal of Structured Finance* and on the editorial advisory board of *American Securitization.*

Index

Printed and bound by CPI Group (UK) Ltd, Croydon, CR0 4YY

23/04/2025

14660904-0001